S0-FJZ-932

DATE DUE

MAR 2 1 '70			
LIBRARY			
U. C.			
APR 2 9 89			
Library			
U. C.			
DEC 14 '92			
LIBRARY			
NOV 2 8 1995			
GAYLORD			PRINTED IN U.S.A.

IN REMEMBRANCE OF ME

IN
REMEMBRANCE
OF ME

By

EDWARD HERBERT REES, S.T.D., A.M.

COKESBURY PRESS

NASHVILLE

IN
REMEMBRANCE
OF ME

DISCARD

By

EDWARD JEFFRIES REES, S.T.B., A.M.

COKESBURY PRESS

NASHVILLE

IN REMEMBRANCE OF ME
COPYRIGHT, MCMXXXII
BY LAMAR & WHITMORE

All rights reserved, including that of translation
into foreign languages, including the Scandinavian

265.3
R25i

SET UP, ELECTROTYPED, PRINTED, AND BOUND
BY THE PARTHENON PRESS AT NASHVILLE
TENNESSEE, UNITED STATES OF AMERICA

C

HUMBLY DEDICATED

IN

LOVING AND TENDER AFFECTION

TO

THOSE TWO FAITHFUL SOULS

WHO

LED THEIR NINE CHILDREN TO SACRAMENTAL ALTARS

MY FATHER AND MOTHER

NOW

IN THEIR HOPEFUL, BECKONING SUNSET DAYS

8241

INTRODUCING THE AUTHOR

THE REVEREND EDWARD JEFFRIES REES is a native of the State of Tennessee. He has the following academic degrees: A.B. from Asbury College, S.T.B. from Boston University School of Theology, and A.M. from Duke University. For the past three years he has been the efficient pastor of the Methodist Episcopal Church, South, in the fine old town of Oxford, North Carolina.

"Of making many books there is no end," and one often wonders why certain books were written, or having been written how they found a publisher. Not so with this book. This is a book that should have been given to the public. And it comes at the right time. The hungry heart of humanity is turning anew to the Bread of Life. The sense of the need of God is finding expression in devout and reverent forms of worship. Spiritually minded men are discovering for themselves the value of the Sacrament of the Lord's Supper. Once again the Living Christ is making himself known in the breaking of the bread. Mr. Rees has ministered wisely to his people. His messages come out of the heart of a faithful pastor. The freshness of a living Christian experience is in this book. The reading of it will prove a blessing to all our people. And I do not doubt that many a pastor will be led through the study of these pages and meditation on these messages to a deeper religious experience and a more useful ministry to his people.

EDWIN D. MOUZON.

CHARLOTTE, NORTH CAROLINA,
NOVEMBER 15, 1931.

CONTENTS

FOREWORD

MY SYMPATHETIC ATTENTION was especially directed to the dignity and beauty of the Sacrament of the Lord's Supper when my Seminary dean, the Reverend James Albert Beebe, A.B., S.T.B., D.D., S.T.D., LL.D., led in a most impressive administration of the Elements in Robinson Chapel, Boston University School of Theology. Since that day my interest in this Service has been intensified, my love for it has been magnified, and my study of it has, to a brief extent, at least, been specialized.

For the reason that the members of my Official Board, and others of the church in which these Communion Addresses have been delivered, have expressed their appreciation of their helpfulness, and their sanction of the order of the Communion Service which followed their delivery, I have been led to publish them, with the humble hope that the inner and increasing significance of this most sacred Sacrament of the Christian Church may be deepened, and yet magnified during these demanding, commanding, fulsome days.

Especially am I indebted to the Reverend Gilbert T. Rowe, A.B., S.T.D., Litt.D., D.D., Professor of Christian Doctrine in the School of Religion of Duke University, Durham, North Carolina, whose constant encouragement led me to place these Addresses in permanent form. Also am I under obligation to the Reverend Frank S. Hickman, A.B., S.T.B., A.M., Ph.D., Professor of the Psychology of Religion in the School of Religion of Duke University, for his valuable suggestions in the preparation of the manuscript. And to Benjamin K. Hays, M.D., noble and learned laymen of my parish, appreciation is due for reading the proof.

11

My thanks are due to Mr. Rudyard Kipling for permission to make quotation from his "Recessional" and "L'Envoi," secured through the courtesy of his publishers, Messrs. A. P. Watt and Son, London; and to Hodder and Stoughton, Ltd., for permission to quote from Jowett's "The Redeemed Family of God." I am indebted to Margaret E. Sangster for permission to quote her poem, "My Tapestry," and to Robert Frost for permission to quote his poem, "Birches."

THE AUTHOR.

THE STUDY,
OXFORD METHODIST EPISCOPAL CHURCH, SOUTH,
OXFORD, NORTH CAROLINA.

I

THE GOSPEL OF ANOTHER CHANCE

THE NEW YEAR ever brings with it the suggestion and opportunity of another chance. Occupying a wing on the third floor of the Montgomery Ward Memorial Building, on the McKinlock Campus of Northwestern University, is a department of the medical school that has come to be known to patients as "the place of another chance."

This is the Department of Physical Therapy, where the maimed and the injured who are financially unable to obtain treatment in a sanatorium are restored to usefulness through the use of heat, water, radiant energy, electricity, massage, and exercise. An average of fifty patients receive treatment each day. They enter this ward with the hopes of another chance.

In a certain State of the Southland "resided" a famous criminal. He had been sent to prison for killing a man. He had escaped, almost miraculously, on three previous occasions. He was placed in "death row." A new Governor came in to preside over the destinies of the State and became interested in this "slippery eel" of a criminal, as he had been termed by the inmates of the penitentiary and by the people of the State. The new Governor said: "I'll make an experiment with this criminal. I'll take him out of 'death row' and give him a job out in the open." The prisoner said: "As long as Governor —— is in office I'll never escape again." That promise was kept—until—the people of the State heard it announced over the radio that "—— had escaped from prison." A reward was offered for his head. He was declared an outlaw. The papers later announced, "Chief of Police of —— and ——, famous criminal, fight duel in daylight on streets of city. The

13

criminal is killed. The Chief is spared. Eleven shots
fired." That criminal had another chance, but he failed to
make good.

The New Year, dawning in its radiant dress, offers to
mankind another chance. Anything which is new possesses
an offer. It carries with it hope. It is a most interesting
experience to read of the "new" things in the Bible. The
Creator, when the world was wrapped in the swaddling
clothes of its infancy, made a division of seasons, time, and
the years. He placed the sun in the sky to announce to
man that it was day. He spun the stars into the heavens,
placed the moon as a near-by companion, and told man that
it was night. He sent the warm breezes or the chilling
breezes of the world's sections to tell to his creation that
"summer approached" or "winter is nigh." The Old Year
came to its close and the New Year to its maternal manger.
Novelty was in the air.

The prophet Isaiah speaks of God creating "*new* heavens
and a *new* earth." But the writer of the Book of Ecclesi-
astes informs us that there is "nothing *new* under the sun."
Yet the Psalmist announces that the Lord "hath put a *new*
song into my mouth," and he proceeds to "sing a *new* song
unto the Lord." In Lamentations we are told that "his
mercies and compassions fail not," and that "they are *new*
every morning." And it is the Christ who, after washing
the disciples' feet—the Service of Humility—proclaims,
"A *new* commandment I give unto you, that ye love one
another." The great Apostle to the Gentiles proclaims,
"If any man be in Christ Jesus, he is a *new* creature: old
things are passed away; all things are created *new*." And
it remains for the penman of the Revelation, who, after he
had looked into other heavens, caused the Creator to say,
"Behold, I make all things *new*."

The crispness of the New Year is appealing; it is beckoning. The Sacrament of the Lord's Supper, administered

and partaken of by God's elect, and by his children at this
particular period and junction of the years, is indeed sol-
emnizing—it is awe-inspiring. I find myself not only particularly conscious of the novelty of the year, but of the
novelty of the Sacrament. The Sacrament is both aged
and novel. Indeed, the Sacrament was the first regular
service of the Church itself. Aged it is! Its date goes
back to a Passover night and to a moonlit Garden, wherein
kneels beneath those ancient, gray, gnarled olive trees the
prostrate, pleading form of God in flesh. It is almost as
aged as Bethlehem's manger. It is of the same age of
Gethsemane's Christ. But—and herewith I make my plea
—is it only an ancient, aged Sacrament! In fact, have we
lost some of the efficacy and worth of the Communion by
stressing its age rather than its effect and power? Have
we not been the poor losers when we have continued to
stress its antiquity, to the neglect of the emphasis upon its
novelty, its modernity, its up-to-dateness? True it is that
it is not in effect "of recent origin," but it is "unusual" in
its novelty. It was, and is, an "innovation" in every sense
of speech.

The Sacrament has belonged too particularly to the "has
been"—to the historical columns of our ritualistic presen-
tations and administrations—rather than to the "it is"—
the current event space, of our lives and the problems,
arising daily, hourly, minutely in connection with those
lives. The ancientness of the Service has been stressed to
the neglect of its modernity. It has been too much on the
old line, when it might, just as appropriately, have been
on the line of newness. We have been satisfied to stand by
the ancient "status quo" of the Supper in its formality and
have done little in the way of pioneering—that pioneering
which would assist the Church in the presentation of the
elements as though they had just been "spilt," and had just
been "broken."

The usual, average administration of the Supper has not "lived on the line of discovery"; rather has it "lived on the line of least resistance." We have gotten through with it quickly—if possible—and pronounced the benediction. We have said by our actions "Veni, Vidi, Vici," and have rested upon the laurels of the Sacrament. We have come, have seen, and acted as though we had conquered, and have been content to abide thereat. But, are there not yet more things in this most sacred Sacrament of the Christian Church that we have not yet discovered?

The peril of the Communion is that it becomes merely a custom, bordering on the line of a hackneyed practice. The danger is that it may become "just another service." It has been too much in a rut; too stationary. It has "remained in one place," taking very little new ground in its glowing application and rich spiritual interpretation. It has, with many of us, as ministers and laymen, been grooved. It is a perilous matter with the Christian Church when this occurs. The fear arises that the sameness of its administration and its reception has sometimes—oftentimes, hindered instead of producing a balm, a healing, a hope within needy hearts, couched in kneeling bodies.

I have found penitent tears lying upon the altar as communicants have partaken of the elements, and have wondered why they were spilt thereon. Was it because of sorrow, or grief? Was it because within the soul of the supplicant there was an aching void? Was it because a confessing prayer had been silently breathed from a sincere heart that the tear was caused to fall? Was it because a holy and inspiring hope had suddenly arisen within a personal breast, causing tears of joy to flow? The tear only silently said to the minister, "Some one needy is bowing here—they want another chance—and they have received another chance at Thine altars."

Henry van Dyke, in his "America for Me," made a rather

interesting, yet, I chance to say, a shockingly truthful observation of dear old Europe, when saying,

> "The past is too much with them
> And the people looking back."

If our looks are only backward in the Communion, we become historic. If they are both backward and forward, we become pioneering and discover new lands in its application. The Lord said to Joshua when he "was old and stricken in years" that "there remaineth yet very much land to be possessed." Indeed, that "land to be possessed" is before the Church of this changing, pioneering century of the world. Thanks for the age of the Sacrament. And thanks for the fact that, like God's mercies, it becomes "new every morning."

When I chance to look about me I discover that novelty is strikingly prominent in Nature. The dewdrop which came, in an endeavor to water the land during the recent drought, which practically covered the nation, was not the same old dewdrop. It was new. It had never watered a perishing bit of grain before. It had never kissed the waiting, parched lips of a drooping flower before. Its journey to this old world was its maiden trip. Others had been here before, but not that very dewdrop. The raindrops which finally followed the drops of nightly dew were novel in their coming. The course from the clouds to the earth had never been made previously by them. Their companions had come and spent themselves in their mission of helpfulness and hope. But these were coming on their initial trip. The falling flakes of snow which gave to so many of our States a "white Christmas" were different flakes from those which had previously drifted so gracefully down to cheer the hearts of happy children and crush the hearts of the poor. When placed under the microscope their diamonds shine out in their beauty of God's other

kinds of gems.   Snowflakes are different; they are novel.
None are alike.   McDowell grasped a wild rose, sensed its
beauty and simplicity, caught its message, and sat down
to give us his appealing lines, "To a Wild Rose."   Other
wild roses had spent their sweetness in almost prodigality
midst flower gardens of rich and poor.   Others had gladdened the hearts of lovers as they walked down by the old
mill stream, and had seen the roses as they bent themselves
over the crooked curves of the rail fences of the South and
the stone fences of New England; but the exact pattern
of McDowell's wild rose had not been before made.   Others
were somewhat alike; none exactly a duplicate.   Novelty,
newness is here.   When Luther Burbank looked in upon
the wild rose he took it and presented it to the flower-loving
world an American Beauty rose; but none have been the
same since the first was made by the hand of God.   And,
in this world of novelty, the Communion makes a strong
appeal to our hearts and minds—that it may not become
fossilized, hemmed in, or crowded.   And I purposed upon
the first Sabbath of my ministry when I administered the
elements not to place it in my mental thinking, or ministe-
rial administration, in the antique shop of the past; but that
it should be presented from time to time to my people as
the most strikingly novel, the most awe-inspiring Sacrament of the Christian Church.

The Communion in the New Year offers the opportunity
of making good.   And, I must not be tardy in my efforts.
For,

> "Our little systems have their day;
>   They have their day and *cease to be:*
>   They are but broken lights of Thee,
> And Thou, O Lord, art more than they."

If we have another chance of making good, of improving
in the days to come, we may rise on stepping stones of

our dead selves to higher things. We may begin again at
Communion altars. We may make a new start. There's
nothing shameful or disgraceful in such an act. Rather
there is something holy in such. The poet evidently realized the privilege of another chance at Christ's altars when
he penned,

> "I wish there were some wonderful place
>   Called the Land of Beginning Again,
> Where all our mistakes and all our heartaches,
>   And all our poor selfish grief,
> Could be dropped like a shabby old coat at the door
>   And never put on again."

There is so much pure gospel in those lines. And, if fail-
ure, in any degree, has crowned or blackened our efforts
during a year just passed, we may get up, grip tightly the
Hand with a nail print in its palm, and start again toward
a better, higher goal—"toward the mark for the prize of
the high calling of God in Christ Jesus."

Again, the communicant is offered the privilege of secur-
ing renewed strength which will assist him in exercising the
Christian virtues. It offers another chance to be true, "for
there are those who trust me"; to be pure, "for there are
those who care." It offers another chance to be strong,
"for there is much to suffer"; a chance to be brave, "for
there is much to dare." It offers a chance to be kind, for
I must "put on kindness"; a chance to be clean, for "clean-
liness is next to godliness." It offers another chance to be
spotless, for the pure in heart "shall see God"; a chance to
be holy, for "I am holy," saith the Lord God of hosts.
It offers another chance to be meek, for "the meek shall
inherit the earth"; to be fair and honest, for "honesty is
the best policy." It offers a chance to be loving, for "char-
ity suffereth long"; and to be kind, for "love is kind"; to
be temperate, for I am told to "be temperate in all things";
and to be faithful, for "faith is the substance of things

hoped for." An opportunity is offered to be diligent, for I must "work, for the night is coming," and "must be about my Father's business"; to be godly, for "godliness with contentment is great gain." Yes, O yes, a rich, fragrant, convincing opportunity is given unto me and mine, unto thee and thine, to approach His altars receiving once more those symbolic elements, as we again dedicate our lives, and receive of His Spirit and strength, so that we may have dominion over sin and strength in temptation's hour. What an Offering! What a Feast! What a Banquet of the soul! Privilege of man beyond compare! Privilege beyond the gift of man! Only God could give such a Gift! Thus, I grasp it. I cherish it. I relish its possession. I glory in its opportunity. I feel the throb of a Voice which spoke upon a Passover night, saying, "Don't forget me." If I do, I'm gone, and nothing but His love and power can ever find me, or bring me back. But, we are pledged to follow Thee!

And, I am offered the privilege of discovering other lands yet to be possessed within the environs of my own soul. The Land of Undiscovered Sacraments, of Unexplored Communions, of the untasted Wine of spiritual edification, of the unbroken and untouched Bread presented for the nourishment of the souls of earth's thirsty and hungry communicants who possess contrite hearts and worshipful spirits. With this in the background of our thinking it will be rather difficult for us to commune in haste, as we try to meet the engagement for a big Sunday dinner on the dot of the hour; for the blessings of the Lord come to those who wait, to those who "tarry a while."

How oft have ministers begged their congregations to "wait—the service will be brief," as some of the richest portions of the ritual were rapidly and carelessly omitted. How oft have ministers implored their congregations to "stay," "not to rush away"; to "be courteous at the Lord's

table, as you would be as a guest in the home of a friend."
Why hurry when we have "the chance of a lifetime" to
kneel again at God's altars and receive just that which is
needed the most in our lives? We have another chance.
"Beloved, now are we the sons of God," said John, "and
it doth not yet appear what we shall be." In such a message there is hope, and the communicant's consecration may
be made. Then, ah!

> "Then into his hand went mine
> And into my heart came He;
> And I walked in a light divine
> The path I had feared to see."

It is in the hope of becoming—becoming something better—that the Christian goes on and on.

It is told that Spurgeon went down into the country to
visit a friend who had built a new barn, and on the barn
was a cupola, upon which had been erected a weather vane
with this text of Scripture on it, "God is love." Spurgeon,
a bit puzzled, asked the man, "What do you mean by put-
ting that text of Scripture on the weather vane? Do you
mean that God's love is as changeable as the wind?" "O
no," was the reply. "I mean to say that God is love,
whichever way the wind blows." Is it not a fact that such
a faith is needed this day? Is it not a fact that Christian
people would be greatly helped, comforted, and inspired
if they should bow at the altar of communion with the
thought, "God is love whichever way the wind blows"?
Facing the New Year, with the spiritual assistance of the
communion, such is our faith and trust and hope.

> "I know not what the future hath
> Of marvel or surprise,
> Assured alone that life and death
> His mercy underlies.

I know not where His islands lift
    Their fronded palms in air;
I only know I cannot drift
    Beyond His love and care."

II

THE UNSEEN HOST

THERE USED TO HANG A MOTTO upon the walls of my childhood home—in fact, it still hangs there—which reads,

> CHRIST IS THE HEAD OF THIS HOME,
> THE UNSEEN GUEST AT EVERY MEAL,
> THE SILENT LISTENER TO EVERY CONVERSATION.

The motto which hangs upon the walls of our parsonage
home declares that "Christ is the *Host* at every meal."
There is a wide margin of difference in being a *guest* and
being a *host*. The guest partakes of the meal prepared
by the host, or hostess. The host is the one who furnishes,
supplies, prepares, makes ready the meal. Christ may be
either a Guest or a Host around our dinner table, but he
distinctly becomes the Host around our Communion table.
Yea, He is the Unseen Host, inviting his friends, his children to "come and dine."

One of the most neglected little spots in Palestine to-day,
but one of the most interesting, is the beckoning town of
Bethany, lying about three miles out from Jerusalem, on
the road to Jericho. There can be seen the fallen stones
of the ruins of the reputed home of Mary, Martha, and
Lazarus. There is shown to the interested visitor the cave
in which Lazarus was buried for several days. One feels
close to the garments of three good souls when stopping in
Bethany. Jesus oft frequented the place, for there lived
some of his most intimate and select friends. He called
upon them when he was in need, and they returned the call.
One day Jesus walked into that little town, and Martha
announced to Sister Mary, "The Master is come, and call-

eth for thee." Dr. Moffatt translates those words by saying, "The Teacher is here, and is calling for you." We
will first consider the presence of the Host.

It is to be really wondered if Christians truly believe that
Christ *is* present in the Sacrament. O, we believe in the
historical presence. Of course, we as Protestants refrain
from believing in the actual presence. Church fathers and
theologians of the yesteryears have come to theological
licks and blows over this very subject. In the early days
of the Christian Church, Christendom was split asunder
over the teaching of the truth, or untruth, of Transubstantiation. We refrain from believing that, through the ritualistic twists of man, the blood and bread of the Sacrament
are changed into the literal blood and body of Christ. But,
haven't we feared so much that we might be called Tran-
substantiationalists, that we have gone almost to the other
extreme in failing to sense the real spiritual presence of
the Christ whose body was broken and whose blood was
spilt for our redemption? Where is there a place that man
can get any closer to the real presence of Christ than at
the Communion altar? It is not a

> ". . . far-off Divine event
> Toward which the whole creation moves,"

but it is the time of all times in Church procedure when it
can be announced from the housetops that "The Master is
here." Martha discovered him in Bethany. We behold
him—we sense his presence—in the Sacrament, and pro-
claim, "He is *here.*" He becomes the Unseen Host.

Many thousands of people had their visions of Christ
clarified and their consecrations renewed when it became
their privilege during the summer of 1930 to gather in that
little city which nestles so coquettishly in the Bavarian
Alps to witness the Passion Play. The motion picture in-

terests of the States became greatly desirous of "screening" the Play. They got into communication with the powers who were playing in that most sacred rendition and pleaded with them to "come to California, and we will screen the play." The reply came back from Bavaria, "We will come, *if you will move our mountain.*" Those who have witnessed the Play know that the natural setting adds greatly to the effectiveness of the rendition. And I am caused to think that Jesus does not have to be removed from Palestine; he does not have to be transported; he is already here. He cannot be bounded by geographical lines and national boundaries. He becomes the Host of the service when the Elements are passed. He is really here, if we have eyes to see. He is really here, if we have ears to hear. He is really here, if we have hearts to receive. Not yonder in an upper room, but here in my Sanctuary. Not yonder with Peter, John, and others, but here with me and mine; with my troubles, cares, burdens; with my joys and victories, and with you and yours.

Day had died in the Nile valley. It was wonderful beyond expression to see the happenings from a train window, and to sense the holy emotions which arose as the Suez Canal was crossed, and the train at Kantara was boarded —the train which would take the travelers to the land of Christ. It was hard to sleep that night, not only on account of the rather poor accommodations of the train, but more so on account of the sacred hush of the hour within our own soul. *Next morning we would awaken in Palestine!* As the pink tints brought the light of day, a choice traveling companion, brushing the sleep from his eyes, remarked, "And to think, this is the land where Christ lived." I found myself replying to my minister friend, "Yes, Christ *was* here, and Christ *is* here." From that early hour we were on a quest for his footprints. When the journey's end came the only subject which presented itself for an address on the Holy Land was, "In His Steps in Palestine." Perfectly truthful and frank, I must confess that many of the so-called designated places where the Master was did not make any appeal to my head or heart. Others did. They hung about me. I could not rid myself of them. I could not if I would. I would not if I could.

After kneeling in the grotto beneath the high altar of the Church of the Nativity in Bethlehem, and after reading the immortal words of Phillips Brooks, which are inscribed there,

> "O little town of Bethlehem,
> How still we see thee lie!
> Above thy deep and dreamless sleep
> The silent stars go by"—

the lines which that matchless preacher conceived when kneeling at that same spot years ago, I walked away with the fact, "The Master is *here,*" ringing within my soul.

Regardless of the crowds, the intense heat, the rivalry which exists between Greek and Roman Catholic Churches as to its exact location, Gethsemane's Garden was entered. Beneath the largest and oldest tree of the Garden, flowers bloomed. A slimy, sleek lizard dared to skirt up the surface of that old tree. Some one said, "That is the tree under which Christ must have prayed." Now, it did not make any particular difference about the exact designation —of the truthfulness or untruthfulness of the "information," but I bent a knee and prayed, "O God, not my will, but Thine be done," and walked out repeating, "The Master is *here.*"

"You know, it seems different *to pray in Nazareth,*" were the words with which another minister and traveling companion greeted me as I walked into our Galilee hotel for the purpose of spending the night. With that thought in mind Nature had her perfect way—for a time. A bit before day a camel train, with tinkling bells, trudged lazily by. In vain I tried to sleep, for I needed it. A bit later the Christ Child seemed to knock at my door and say, "Get up, walk out with me." I obeyed, and sat alone "when purple morning breaketh" on a hillside on the outskirts of Nazareth, beholding those hills over which the Child romped and played. A little stream ran slowly and impressively by. "Did He ever go wading in that? Did He ever sail any boats in there?" The Virgin's Fountain was later reached, declared to be one of the most exact locations of historic significance in Palestine to-day, and there His little barefoot, smiling, youthful presence was sensed. Again, it must be said, "The Master is *here*."

Go with me to Galilee.

> "O Galilee, blue Galilee,
> Where Jesus loved so much to be,"

were the words in song which floated over the peaceful surface of the lake whereon He walked, and beside whose shores He preached His greatest sermons. Was He there; really there? Could one "believe his eyes"? But, when

> "Galilee's sun was westering
> And Galilee's waves were whispering on the strand,"

again it was confessed within and without, "The Master is *here*." And it can be said, in all fairness and truthfulness, that if it is possible for a modern pilgrim to Palestine to sense the spiritual presence of the Galilean along its shores, lakes, and borders, surely in the broken bread and spilt wine of His life we can feel that He is not far away; that He is near; that

> "Closer is He than breathing,
> And nearer than hands and feet."

No, Jesus not only came into Bethany; he comes into my village, town, city. Nay, Jesus did not only come into the hospitable confines of the home of Lazarus, but he walks into the portals of my home. No, no, Jesus not only broke bread with the disciples on a darkened, hysterical night, but he breaks bread around my family table, around the Communion Board. "The Master is here," surely so! But let us see the latter part of the text: "He *calleth* for thee."

No doubt, Jesus' postponement of his visit to Bethany rather puzzled Mary and Martha. They were in trouble and wanted help. They were lonesome and wanted consolation. They were close enough to him to personally seek his consolation. They had not merely waited until the day was dark to call upon him, but had previously manifested their loyalty, devotion, and fealty when their day was bright. They were not calling upon him only in the hour of emergency. They were too fair for that. But they did think that it was proper to send for Jesus in their sad hour, when their brother, the only brother, as far as we know—"when he whom thou lovest is sick." But Jesus waited two days and then answered the call, stating to his disciples before his arrival—*after the burial*—"I was glad for your sakes that I was not here, to the intent ye may believe." When his arrival in Bethany was known, Martha spoke, saying, "If thou hadst been here, my brother had not died." Jesus immediately promised her that her brother would rise again. She came back with the intelligent and faithful answer, "He shall rise in the resurrection."

Just at this place the Master took the opportunity of teaching, not only that "I am the *resurrection*," but that the blessing which may be expected and sought in the to-morrow may be had in the to-day. "I *am* myself resurrection and life" is Moffatt's translation. The emphasis is upon the verb, "I am." Jesus, in his raising of Lazarus from the dead, taught that resurrections are possible to-day —now—any time that the faithful soul may wish to claim

them through Christ's name. The Teacher did not say that
he "would be" or "was going to be" resurrection and life,
but that on that very day, in Bethany, among his friends
in need, he *was* resurrection. He said to the mournful,
almost-hopeless women, who would have been entirely
hopeless had they not sent for Jesus, "Do you seek a
resurrection? If so, the Resurrection is here *this* day.
Open your eyes and behold Me—I *am* life."

The rather interesting thing about this conversation is
that Christ declared himself to be the Resurrection *before*
the day of his arising. Faithful devotees of the Nazarene
knew and believed that his words would be fulfilled—in
some way or another. They were not convinced as to the
manner, but they held, in a large majority, the hope "eternal in the human breast," that Christ would arise, that he
would be resurrection and life to them. But, as for his
being resurrection and life *before* Golgotha, why, that had
not occurred to them. Jesus announced himself to be the
Bread of life *before* his body was broken; and with the
announcement he proceeded to distribute the Bread. He
announced himself to be the Water of life *before* the stream
proceeded from Calvary. He announced himself to be the
Light of the world *before* the rays of the rising sun of
Resurrection's morn proclaimed him to be the Light of the
world, by which we may light our flickering torches. A
writer of distinct spiritual note has declared that "revelations are made in the closet which are made nowhere else."
These revelations had been made known to Christ in the
closet of his own experiences, but he proclaimed them to
a world which was rather slow in understanding the truth
which he presented.

Thus, we need not live on the line of postponement.
Many of the choicest blessings of life never come to us
because we postpone their reception, thinking that they will
surely come to us in a later hour, a future day. We need

not wait in the breadlines of hunger when the Bread is ready for distribution to-day. We need not wait in the shadows of moroseness and gloom, when the wine of gladness has been provided for our spiritual edification to-day. No, we need not be Christians in the Gloom, but Christians in the Glow. We need not wait for the Water of life to course down our way some day in the far-off, but to-day its life-giving streams flow by our heart's door. And in the flowing of this stream the Master calleth for me. Even so, need we not wait for heaven to come, when it is here to-day—this very day—within my heart, and the heart of my fellow Christians. Those who walk with faith will attain it now.

> "He who walks in love may wander far,
> Yet God will bring him where the blessed are."

More and more do we receive consolation in knowing that heaven begins here. We need not wait till we get to heaven to see Jesus; he is here in the quiet, peaceful, hopeful face of my mother, and the smiling faces of my children. I once had a pastor, who was not known to be the most scholarly minister in his Conference. He was not known as the greatest pulpiteer. But no man outshone him in devotion and consecration. When he preached, the greatest sermon was his life. It was holy, and the members of his flock knew of its holiness. But I saw Jesus in him. I saw heaven in him. I received a bit of heaven from him.

Eternal streams are within us *now*. Heavenly dividends are payable now. "Moment by moment" do they come. Eternal life is within us at this hour. We need not wait till death knocks and the committal is said by the minister. "Whosoever liveth and believeth in me shall *never* die." Life begins at the point where faith begins. It ceases when faith stops. Jesus said, "Whoso eateth my flesh, and drinketh my blood, *hath* eternal life." There was no futurity in such a statement. The eternal life begins with the eating and drinking of Him. This thought changes the "Grim Reaper" to the "Happy Gardener." This changes the "cold, dark, chilly stream" to the hopeful, beckoning "river of life."

Then, ah then, I will lease a lot in Paradise to-day, this glorious day. I shall not live in the to-morrows, but I shall thrive in the gladsome to-days. No, I definitely refuse, of my own free will and accord, to live on the line of postponement, but I shall claim my resurrection to-day, basing my simple faith upon Him who proclaimed Himself to be the Resurrection of the present, as well as of the future. The eagerness of my soul rises within me, causing me to declare dividends this very day, this glorious day of my faith. "The Master calleth for thee." I hear! I respond! It is with such a conviction, hope, and trust that we may again partake of the elements of love, sacrifice, and devotion. The unseen Host is present, presiding over His most sacred Table.

The greatest organ in Europe was safely and carefully kept by an aged man. The keeper was almost painfully particular with regard to the one who might use that instrument of beauty and wonder. One day a strange young man walked into the cathedral where rested the organ and asked the privilege of playing on its board. The keeper announced to him that the organ was very valuable and that only the highly selected artists might have a chance upon it. The strange young man begged. He insisted. He persisted until the aged keeper reluctantly extended to him the key which would unlock the organ. Sitting down, in utter faith and composure, the young man began to run up and down the keys of the great instrument. The keeper listened. The stranger played on. The storm could be heard, and the waves began to toss as he played. The winds were heard to moan, and the thunders rolled.

The storm ceased, and the birds were heard to sing, and the organist ceased his playing. "But," said the keeper in almost dumb surprise, "who are you?" Modestly the young organist replied, "I am Felix Mendelssohn." Ah! the great, distinguished composer had come! That made a difference. And S. D. Gordon remarks, "Every man is a music box; but only the Master can unloose the music within a life." The holiest Sacrament within the gift of God, administered by the failing, faltering hands of man, consecrated as those hands may be, offers the penitent communicant the opportunity of tuning his life to the life of Christ. And, after the tuning, the music will come. At Thine altars the discords are removed. The flats are changed. Man is made into a music box for God.

> "Too soon we rise: the symbols disappear;
>   The feast, though not the love, is past and gone;
>   The bread and wine remove: *but thou art here,*
>   Nearer than ever—still my shield and sun."

III

THE DUAL ELEMENT IN THE COMMUNION

THE CALAMITY OF THE COMMUNION is its commonness; made so by a careless spirit which may manifest itself in its administration and its reception. The glory of the Communion is that it may be "new every morning." The hope of the Communion is in its helpfulness, made so by the hand of God, assisted by the hand of man.

The wealth of the Communion is in its price, while the solace of the Communion is in its cure. The strength of the Communion is in its power, while the poise of the Communion is in its peace. The width of the Communion is the world. The breadth of Communion is man's need; while its romance is its reach. It is toward the width, breadth, and the romance of the Sacrament that our minds are now directed.

One of the Synoptic writers informs us that "the blood is shed for YOU," and that "my body is given for YOU." The other two writers state that "my blood is shed for MANY." The first writer's statement is personal. The statement of the other two implies universality. Yet the statements of all three writers are both personal and universal. It would have been a calamity had Christ died only for the disciples. It would have been a tragedy had his death been only for Palestinians. He died for Peter, but he also died for me. He spilt his blood for John, and his body was broken for Judas, but the shedding of his life's blood, and the breaking of his body was for America, for Africa, for India, for the whole world.

We have heard much talk within the decade just closing relative to a social gospel. And I am in harmonious agreement with all the charitable and philanthropic elements of the appeals of the social gospel. We have heard much preaching relative to a militant gospel; and I am sure that Zion must be ever busily and heroically engaged in a militant encounter of right versus wrong. But in all of this emphasis have we not swung away from the personal gospel? In the light of the communion we must present a personal gospel. His blood was shed for *me*—for *you*. It is encouraging to note during these days, however, the long list of books coming from the press of our churches on the subject of "Christian Experience" as applied personally.

I am standing alone before the cross "on a hill far away." I hear the expressions of forgiveness and love which flow from the lips of the Crucified. It has been stated that Christ would have gone to the cross as gladly and as willingly for one soul as he went there for the souls of the world. I can receive, and do receive a keen bit of consolation from that thought. He dropped his head on a pulseless breast for *me*. His blood was spilt for *me*. His side was pierced for *me*. His head was crowned with thorns for *me*. His sinless, stainless body was broken for *me*. And then I go on and say that He arose for *me*. His prayers to-day are for *me*. He makes earnest intercession for *me*.

Religion is suffering among us to-day for the reason that we have so largely lost the individual application of the claims and the appeal of the gospel message. The Book of Jonah has truthfully been called "the John Three Sixteen of the Old Testament," in its missionary teaching. But, when I read that "God so loved the *world*," I know that I am included in that love, and in that sacrifice. And I ask myself, "Why should his body be broken for *me?* Why should his blood be spilt for *me?*" I have done nothing worthy. I have done nothing which would merit that sacrifice. A young preacher of Japanese birth came to

America in search of a college education, which was Christian through and through. His walk among his classmates was a lowly, holy walk. His life was genuine. His consecration was challenging. With diploma in hand he set sail for his native land. After a few years of work in Japan he wrote back to his classmate, saying, "God's goodness *shames* me." And surely it does! His goodness applied personally toward *me!*

The horror of the early Christians was not martyrdom, but disloyalty. They almost courted the headman's ax. The block was a challenge to them to be worthy of Christ's sacrifice and his goodness. No conscientious Christian can stand reverently and thoughtedly upon the small slab in the square of Florence and read the inscription which tells of the strangulation and burning of Savonarola, and later visit the Church of the Duomo where he preached so fearlessly against the sins of his day in high and low places, without feeling that that noble apostle of a personally applied religious freedom and Christian experience must have felt the strong personal application of the merits of the Sacrament within his own spotless soul. He must have felt, as a studious young monk, the truth of the teaching of "This is my body which was given for *you*—my blood which was shed for *you*." And in gracious gratitude, I partake of the elements which were shed and broken for *me*. They are personally applied.

> "Have you read that He looked to heaven and said,
>   ''Tis finished'? 'Twas for *thee!*
> Have you ever said, 'I thank Thee, Lord,
>   For giving Thy life for *me*'?"

But the record says that His blood was shed "for many." It was an inclusive shedding. It was an inclusive breaking of bread. In these days, when missions are being criticized at home and abroad by friend and foe, there lies a very salient missionary emphasis in the Sacrament. That teaching has always been there, but possibly not emphasized. To omit the universal element in the Sacrament is suicidal to missions. I have a friend in the Congo, doing missionary work among some very backward Africans. As he administers the Sacrament to them he tells them that Christ's blood was "shed for many." Another friend is in Burma, another in China, another in Korea, others in India, Java, and elsewhere. When these friends of college days pass the bread and wine to natives with upturned faces and upturned hearts they are consoled in the knowledge that the Sacrifice on Golgotha's heights was for people of all races, of all colors, of any and all climes. Christ did not shed his blood for a select few, for the people of a so-called high strata of society; not only for the outcasts of India, but the stream flowed down and down until to-day its reach is to the far outposts of civilization.

Dr. Stephen Corey tells of the time when the Mission Board sent out a fine young medical missionary, in the person of Zenas Loftis, to a station on the border of Tibet, in West China. Young Loftis traveled with his Chinese guides for more than four months across Central China. His travel was made in a house boat, in wheelbarrows, sedan chairs, on the back of a yak, and on foot. He crossed mountains and went around dangerous precipices on the backs of Chinese coolies. As he was scaling the last great mountain pass before reaching his destination, he passed a lone mail carrier coming east. He hastily scribbled the following lines and sent them back: "I am so glad you did not stop me down in the interior of China, but sent me 'way up here on the roof of the world, where the people are so much more the bond servants of sin, that I might be used in the most needy and difficult spot in all the world." When that pioneering young missionary arrived in that distant field it was with the message: "Christ's blood was shed for *many*."

But so many have been omitted from the Communion. It isn't the fault of the plan, or institution of the Sacrament. The One who administered the initial sacramental service knew that it was for, and must be for, the nations of the earth. Christ knew that the Sacrament which he was instituting on that darkened, eventful night must not be circumscribed. When religion is circumscribed, it loses. If we want to kill religion, let us hasten and tie it to its home base. If we would murder it, confine it. If we would stifle it, bottle it up. If we would smother it, cover it with the blanket of its native shores. If we would render it powerless, confine it to a home policy. If we would clip the wings of religion, prevent it from flying beyond its own confines into other environs. If we would discourage religion, fence it in. If we would bury the hopes of a needy world, fail to obey the last command and great commission, "Go ye." For religion without philanthropy is dry bones. If religion would find its life, it must lose its life. Religion loses by retention. It gains by presentation. Religion halts by blindness. It advances through vision. Religion expands by sacrifice. It retracts by cowardice. Religion without a "Go ye" becomes a religion of the "Stay ye." Religion of the "home base" will eventually become a religion of a "no base." Religion propagated develops a civilization Christianized. Religion emasculated is on the way to the cemetery. The Christianity of the Communion rail is the Christianity of pioneering, expanding crusades. The Christianity of the Sacramental altar possesses that element of universality which will eventually, in the name of Him who said to his disciples upon one of those few occasions upon which he spoke of his Church, "The gates of hell shall not prevail against it," encompass the world and bring it to the pierced feet of Him who with pierced bleeding hands said, "This is my blood which *is shed for many*." It is really in that faith, and such a faith alone, that the elements can be consistently and faithfully distributed to the communicants of the world—those bowing at mahogany altars in our most beautiful temples of worship—those bowing in the tall grass of Africa and other mission outposts, who receive the Sacrament from the hands of God's pioneering souls on the far-flung mission lines of Christianity's conquering cause.

The late and lamented Bishop Theodore S. Henderson, during the height of his effective evangelistic crusades and constructive ministry, told of receiving a rather peculiar parcel post package in the post office of the small county seat town wherein was located the seat of the Conference college. With peculiar thoughts and wonderment the bishop proceeded to open his package, finding it to be some grape juice and a loaf of bread. These were accompanied with the written request from a mountain missionary of Kentucky: "We want to have the first Communion service the people in this section have ever witnessed. Not possessing the proper credentials and ordination from the Church, we hereby request that you consecrate the elements, and return the same to us." These words were the contents of that reasonable request. Said the bishop, "At a midnight hour in my hotel room I went through the entire service of consecration contained in the ritual of the Discipline, and on next morning I mailed the elements back to the mountain missionary. God was present in that room, and I was touched to tears to think that those unfortunates of that section of Kingdom Come would have the privilege of receiving their first communion." Yes, through the ritualistic services of Christendom we consecrate the elements, but in the rank informality of that Upper Room on a darkened night the provision was made for all mankind to "take and eat"; to "drink ye all of it"; to drink "my blood of the New Testament, which is shed for *you* and for *many,* for the remission of sins."

In the light of this incident, and in the truth of the stories which appear weekly in the columns of Church papers, relating the experiences of missionaries in the home and foreign lands, as they tell of the eagerness with which natives, and others, beg for the Bread of life, my experience of religion will not allow me to remain complacent. I cannot remain comfortable. It comforts me when I know that the blood and body are "for me"; but the comforting touch is nearly gone when I turn and read "for many," as I know that the average Christian is doing pitifully little, if anything at all, which would assist in the distribution of the Bread to others beyond the seas. Communion is not a panacea—a "pretended remedy for all diseases"; but the efficacy of the provisions are such that a healing balm may be applied to earth's sorrows—all sorrows; for "earth has no sorrow that Heaven cannot heal."

In such a frame of mind, and with faith, I carefully planned a Missionary Communion Service. Offering plates were placed at convenient locations within the chancel. The accustomed invitation to Communion was given, with emphasis upon those portions which carry unusual missionary teachings and enthusiasms, such as:

> "Judge of *all men.*"
> "Have mercy upon us—*Father.*"
> "Promised forgiveness of sins *to all them.*"
> "Suffer death for *our redemption.*"
> "Who made a full—sacrifice for sins of—*whole world.*"
> "Take—eat—my body—given for *you.*
> "This is my blood—shed for *many.*"
> "Thy *Kingdom* come."

A similar communion meditation as this herewith presented was given. The request was made that the communicants bring with them to the Sacramental Table their offerings of love and missionary interest, and after communing, place them in the offering plate. My eyes saw kneeling for the reception of the bread and wine a host of people who were connecting within their own minds and hearts the Sacrament and Missions. It was for them, and for many others, seen and unseen, at home and abroad, scattered throughout the world, for which Christ had died, that the Last Supper was instituted. It was with "Remember me" that they knelt, prayed, and supped again. It was with "Go ye" that they coöperated in that service. It was with "Send me" that they partook of the broken elements; and it was with "Prove me" that they offered themselves and their possessions again for the eventual redemption and Christianization of humankind of all classes and climes.

IV

THE CHALLENGE OF THE CHALICE

"Earth's crammed with heaven,
And every common bush afire with God;
But *only he who sees* takes off his shoes—
The rest sit round and pluck blackberries."

So SPOKE THIS WRITER of wholesome lines, and truths eternal. No doubt Elizabeth Barrett Browning would be a bit surprised were she to know that a minister of the gospel should quote her lines, applying them to the Communion. But such is the case. "Only he who sees" may understand the appeal of the Cup, the challenge of the Chalice.

The Sacrament of the Lord's Supper has been with the followers of Christ since the incipiency of the Christian Church. But how many of the modern devotees of Christ have seen that this Sacrament is "crammed full" with meaning—so full that we have not yet plumbed its depths? Has not the day arrived for Protestant Christianity—for the Christianity of the world—to discover and teach some of the deeper, broader, richer, holier, keener meanings of this Feast of the soul? Indeed it is a Symbol, but more than a symbol. It is a Feast, but more. It is a Sacrament, yet more. It is a Memorial, but too long has the Church been content to allow this service to remain in the section of memoirs among the chapters of Church history—and more pitifully and pathetically true, in the field of Christian experience. The Church has taught much relative to its antiquity, and not enough upon its cure for iniquity. The Sacrament has remained too long among the antiques in the museums of bygone days, and has not been applied

41

sufficiently to the transgressions in the abiding places of these to-days. In order to evaluate this Sacrament of Christendom and place it in closer touch with the appeals, needs, and problems of a modern day there must be a two-fold look: One which looks backward; another which looks onward. A certain fire insurance company of London advertises in these words, "Tested by the fires of two centuries." This service of Christendom has been tested by the fires of practically twenty centuries. It has stood the test. Will it stand the test of the oncoming centuries? It has stood the strains of the yesteryears; will it meet the demands of the to-morrows? That depends upon its interpretation and application to the needs and requirements of those unborn days which yet rest within the womb of the oncoming centuries.

The infant church established her "sacraments" and presented them to the world. They were interpreted and defined from various angles. Augustine's definition of a sacrament was, "The visible form of an invisible grace." As a result of the Council of Trent, which met in 1547, the number of sacraments was fixed at seven—namely, Baptism, Confirmation, the Eucharist, Penance, Extreme Unction, Orders, and Matrimony. The divergence of the Protestant Churches from this decision was based upon the fact that these proceeded on no settled principles. The notion that there are seven sacraments has no New Testament authority and must be described as purely arbitrary. It is perfectly arbitrary, for example, to place Baptism and the Lord's Supper, which were instituted by Christ as ordinances of the Church, in the same category with marriage, which rests not on His appointment but on a natural relationship between the sexes that is as old as the human race. While, therefore, the Reformers retained the term "sacrament" as a convenient one to express the general idea that has to be drawn from the characteristics of the rites classed together under this name, they found the distinguishing marks of the sacraments (1) in their institution by Christ, (2) in their being enjoined by him upon his followers, and (3) in their being bound up with his word and revelation in such a way that they become "the expressions of Divine thoughts, the visible symbols of Divine acts." As Baptism and the Lord's Supper are the only two rites for which such marks can be claimed, it follows that there are only two New Testament sacraments. A justification for their being classed together under a common name may be found in the way in which they are associated in the New Testament. Note the association, the description being given of the day of Pentecost, "Then they that gladly received his word were baptized . . . and they continued steadfastly in the apostles' doctrine and fellowship, and in breaking of bread." (Acts 2: 41, 42. See also 1 Cor. 10: 1-4.)

The statement just made, that both Baptism and the Lord's Supper owe their origin as sacraments of the Church to their definite appointment by Christ himself, has been strongly challenged by some modern critics. We will deal only with the latter. This challenge rests mainly upon the fact that the saying, "This do in remembrance of me," is absent from the Mark and the Matthew texts and is found only in the Supper-narratives of Paul (1 Cor. 11: 24, 25) and his disciple Luke (Luke 23: 19). Upon this circumstance large structures of critical hypotheses have been reared. It has been affirmed that in the upper room Jesus was only holding a farewell supper with his disciples, and that it never occurred to him to institute a feast of commemoration. It has been further maintained that the views of Jesus regarding the speedy consummation of his kingdom make it impossible that he should have dreamed of instituting a sacrament to commemorate his death. The significance of the feast was eschatological merely; it was a pledge of a glorious future hour in the perfected kingdom of God. And the theory has been advanced that the institution of this sacrament as an ordinance of the Church designed to commemorate Christ's death was due to the initiative of Paul, who is supposed to have been influenced in this direction by what he had seen in Corinth and elsewhere of the mystery-practices of the Greek world.

All these hypothetical fabrics fall to the ground, of course, if the underlying assumption that Jesus never said, "This do in remembrance of me," is shown to be unwarrantable. And it is unwarrantable to assume that a saying of Jesus which is vouched for by Paul and Luke cannot be authentic because it does not occur in the corresponding narratives of Matthew and Mark. *The validity and authenticity of a truth does not necessarily depend upon the oft repetition of that truth.* In these narratives, which are highly compressed in any case, the first two evangelists would seem to have confined themselves to setting down those sayings which formed the essential moments of the Supper and gave it symbolic contents. The command of its repetition they may have regarded as sufficiently embodied and expressed in the universal practice of the Church from its earliest days. For as to that practice there is no question. (Acts 2: 42-46; Acts 20: 7; 1 Cor. 10: 16 and 11: 26.)

The storms have blown upon this sacramental Feast. The slits and splits have come in the adoption of this Service. But, thanks be to God, the knits have come, and they are still coming. (See Chapter V, "The Family of Christ.") It has been whacked, hacked, and attacked, but the faithful ones of to-day track to these solemn altars. It has been tramped upon, and trampled over, but untrammeled souls partake of its holy influence and power. It has been minimized by some, and by others ostracized and scandalized, but still its efficacy holds. That the Holy

Spirit has brooded over this Memorial is the explanation. The same Spirit who guided the Church in the determination of the Canon of the New Testament Scriptures, the same Spirit who directed the Church in the working out of the explicit formulation of the Christian doctrine of the Godhead, and of the Christ—that selfsame Spirit led the Church in the formation and fashioning of her great eucharistic prayer into its norm in the same fourth century.

The historic Churches of the East, by their faithful adherence to this norm, have been almost undisturbed by the dissensions and disputes of Western Christendom touching the Eucharist. The glimpses given us in the earlier Fathers of the Eucharist are in entire accord with the more articulate expression of the Church's corporate eucharistic worship, which we find in the liturgical documents and writings of the Nicene era. Justin Martyr tells us that the Eucharist was celebrated on the Lord's Day. Irenæus emphasizes the fact that Christ taught his disciples to offer the new oblation of the New Covenant, to present in thank-offering the first-fruits of God's creatures—bread and wine—the pure sacrifice prophesied before by Malachi. Offerings of a spiritual and a material nature are quite appropriate at Communion altars. (See Chapter III, "The Dual Element in the Communion.") Cyprian, too, gives evidence to the same eucharistic belief and alludes very plainly to the "Lift up your hearts," in the great thanksgiving.

Originally the Apostolic Church celebrated Communion at every meeting for worship. They "continued steadfastly in the apostles' teaching and fellowship, in the breaking of bread," and in prayers. Very soon, however, if we are to judge from the Acts and the Pauline epistles, its administration was confined to the meeting on the first day of the week. Doctrines of the Eucharist began to develop. The Romish Church couches its doctrine in the word "transubstantiation," which means the conversion of the substance of the elements used in the Eucharist. The word was first used by Hildebert of Tours in a sermon. The doctrine of the Supper was finally fixed, together with the new term, by Pope Innocent III, at the Lateran Council in 1215 A.D. It was decided that the body and the blood of Christ are truly contained in the sacrament of the altar, under the species of bread and wine, the bread being transubstantiated into the body and the wine into the blood of Christ, by the Divine power. This has been the Romish doctrine of the Supper ever since.

The Reformers rejected the doctrine of transubstantiation, the sacrificial conception of the Eucharist, the adoration of the "host," the withholding of the cup, the efficiency of the Eucharist in behalf of the dead, and the entire Romish conception of the sacrament of the Supper. The original position of Luther, that the elements were signs and seals of the remission of sins, was soon replaced by the doctrine of "consubstantiation." He placed himself squarely on the realistic conception of the words of the institution, and held that "the body of Christ is in accordance with the will and omnipotence of God, and its own ubiquity is really and substantially present *in, with,* and *under* the Supper, even as His divine nature is in the human as warmth is in the iron. This doctrine is to this day the view of the Lutheran Church.

Zwingli differed with Luther. He interpreted the words of the institution—"that is"—as signifying "this stands for," "this signifies." Reduced to its last analysis, the eucharistic concept of Zwingli is that the Supper is a *symbolical* memorial of the suffering and death of Christ, although he does not deny that Christ is present to the eye of faith. In the Supper we confess our faith, we express what that faith means to us, and we do it in memory of Christ's death. The Zwinglian view has been consciously or unconsciously adopted by a very large portion of the Protestant Church.

Calvin's position tends rather to the Lutheran than to the Zwinglian view. With Zwingli the Sacrament is little more than a sign; with Calvin, it is both a sign and a seal. The reality of communion with Christ and the benefits of his death, received by a living faith—all this is common in the Lutheran and the Calvinistic views. The Lord's Supper is far more than a memorial service; it is a marvelous means of grace as well. The central thought of the Calvinistic conception of the Supper is this: The communicant, through the operation of the Holy Spirit, comes into spiritual contact with the entire person of Christ, and is thus fed unto life eternal.

In the historic "Articles of Religion" of the Methodist Church we sense the opinion and interpretation of that great Founder, Rev. John Wesley, M.A. In the paragraph given over to the Sacraments it is stated: "There are two sacraments ordained of Christ our Lord in the Gospel; that is to say, Baptism and the Supper of the Lord. Those five commonly called sacraments; that is to say, Confirmation, Penance, Orders, Matrimony, and extreme Unction, are not to be counted for Sacraments of the Gospel, being such as have partly grown out of the corrupt following of the apostles. . . . The Sacraments were not ordained of Christ to be gazed upon, or to be carried about; but that we should duly use them. And in such only as worthily receive the same, they have a wholesome effect or operation." What a challenge to the ministry, the administrators at Communion altars, to endeavor to the utmost of their mental and spiritual powers to see that the Sacrament may "have a wholesome effect"! What a challenge to communicants to partake "worthily" in order that the elements and the devotion may "have a wholesome effect"! Article XVIII clearly states that "The Supper of the Lord is not only a sign of the love that Christians ought to have among themselves one to another, but rather is a sacrament of our redemption by Christ's death: insomuch, that to such as rightly, worthily, and with faith receive the same, the bread which we break is a partaking of the body of Christ; and likewise the cup of blessing is a partaking of the blood of Christ. . . . The sacrament of the Lord's Supper is not by Christ's ordinance reserved, carried about, lifted up, or worshiped." No, we do not worship the Supper, but the Christ whose life and death are remembered in the Supper.

Having taken this brief observation of the establishment and history of the development of sacramental interpretations, it becomes opportune for our faces to be turned toward the present and the days beyond, as this Feast is yet to be spread and administered. The parchments which bear the record of my ordination as an elder in the Methodist Church carry the date of September 21, 1921. That was an unusually holy hour to me. It had been looked forward to with ripe expectancy and beckoning hope. The weight of the episcopal hand, together with the weight of the hands of the other elders, and a personal friend with whom I had begun my ministry, can yet be felt. But more than the weight of their hands was the warmth of Another hand, the hand of the Holy Spirit. When these ordination parchments were given into my possession I cherished them, and, like many other ministers, had them framed, hanging them upon the walls of my study. But another experience was yet to come.

Methodism practices two ordinations: the ordination of deacons, and the ordination of elders. The ordination as a deacon in the Church gives the minister authority to do two things. The bishop's words are these: "Take thou authority to execute the office of a deacon in the Church of God"; "Take thou authority to read the Holy Scriptures in the Church of God." The Methodist Church has thought it wise and prudent to withhold the power to administer the Sacrament as a Deacon.[1] Thus the bishop says to the candidate for deacon's orders, "It appertaineth to the office of a deacon to *assist* the elder—especially when he ministereth the holy communion." The candidate for elder's orders is asked, "Will you give your faithful diligence, always . . . to administer the doctrines and *sacraments* . . . as the Lord hath commanded?" The ordination prayer is offered, "The Lord pour upon thee the Holy Ghost for the office and work of an elder in the Church of God. . . . Be thou a faithful dispenser of the word of God, and of his *holy sacraments*." With the Bible delivered into the hands of the candidate, by the bishop, he says, "Take thou authority to preach the word of God, and to administer the *holy sacrament* in the congregation." Methodism has not erred in withholding the authority to administer the Sacrament by her ministers until they have been fully ordained. She, considering the Sacrament as the holiest service of the Church, has seen that her ministers were worthy and well qualified before full powers were placed in their hands. And she has done well!

With the glow of this ordination in my heart, I received my appointment, and in Methodist fashion, I was off to my new field. It had been determined by me to place everything possible of a mental and a spiritual nature into the sacramental service. Imagine my sorrow when it was noticed that one of the most faithful stewards, keen lawyer he was, present on Communion Sunday, did not partake. This steward was interviewed, and kindly asked, "Why is it that you do not partake of the Sacrament?" Sense the shock which came, with an accompanying sadness, when he said, "To tell you frankly, *I don't think there's much to it.*"

[1] Preachers in charge, though not ordained, may now administer baptism and the Sacrament of the Lord's Supper in the absence of an elder or bishop.

A most devoted soul in another congregation always absented herself from church on Communion Sunday, but was present on other Sundays, coöperating in every way possible. Another great heart in yet another congregation regularly absents himself from Communion altars. There are just or unjust reasons for this being true. However, the words of that steward came, not only as a shock, but as a challenge—namely, to see that "there's much to it." Illustrations as these can be received by untold hundreds of ministers if a "poll" on the subject were sent out. It was encouraging to notice that on subsequent Communion services my steward was present and devoutly communed.

Yet, the question must be placed, and it remains for Christendom to answer it: How much of careful thought, faithful planning, and devout prayers have gone into the *preparation* for Communion, that this service might be the most efficacious sacrament, the highest and holiest joy of every humble follower of Him who instituted this Meal upon a darkened, beastly night? John Huss went to the flames crying for the cup to be given to the laity. Christ's blood was spilt that His life might be spread. His body was broken that His cross might be borne. Parched lips must be watered, and famishing souls must receive nourishment. The Sacrament is the Answer. More than nineteen hundred years have passed since the night of its institution. By the aid of priceless parchments and manifold manuscripts, it has been traced step by step back through the centuries in unbroken continuity. Whatever the modern church might do to attract the attention of disinterested minds, and command the devotion of lukewarm hearts, may be happily received. A foremost Methodist minister is now working on a plan for the sacrament to be administered to the large congregations which wait upon his ministry, as the people remain in their pews, in order that time may be conserved. It is not the *place* where Communion is received, but the *purpose* of its reception. It is not the physical *posture* in its acceptance, but the spiritual *poise* in its acceptance which is important. The Sacrament has belonged too long to the "Committee on Memoirs" and not enough to the "Committee on Spiritual State (and Christian Interpretation) of the Church." Constant application of the powers of the Church to the demands and commands of this Service will assist in solving this problem, which presents a challenging need. In these days of Pentecostal celebrations, as we work on this problem, it might be helpful constantly to bear in mind that there is a very intimate relationship existing between the Supper room and the Upper room.

In a later chapter (Chapter IX, "A Study in Art") somewhat is said relative to Leonardo da Vinci's masterpiece, "The Last Supper." Imagine the disappointment of a pilgrim to the city wherein is located this painting of world renown to find that admittance to the refectory of the aged building could not be gained, because it was a feast day, and all business houses, and public places, except the churches, were closed. An extra price was offered by generous Americans who had their hearts set upon the feast which this painting would provide for them. I had desired to bathe my imagination, and to cleanse my soul, in its awe-inspiring majesty, wonder, and hope—despite its fading shades. But alas! it was behind closed doors, it could not be looked upon on that feast day. We missed it, with deep regret. *Is not this Sacrament behind closed doors in the minds and hearts of many followers of Christ to-day?* We do not see it as it is, as it was instituted. Other hindrances have crept in. The original which Jesus painted in an upper room has faded before the eyes of our memories. Not only have our visions suffered, but our hearts have lost. The feasts have been on, and the real Feast has been passed by. The interpretation of its significance has been too much restricted. It has been narrowed down. We have not paused sufficiently long to bathe our souls in its power, or to seek its poise. We have rushed by. We have abbreviated. The Elder has too often been "straitened for time." The feasts of other services in the church have been of more (?) consequence and importance! Other services have been more interesting and have drawn larger crowds. The truths of this Sacrament have been hidden, and the masses have passed by—without seeing and—without receiving. These fulsome days, with their demands, have crowded its meaning out. We have witnessed the grim externals of this Sacrament, but have passed on without basking our souls in the sunlight of its internal—and eternal—interpretations. The Sacrament behind closed doors! If the doors are closed—the doors to its inner secrets—who shall open them? Shall Protestantism? Shall Methodism? Shall your Church and mine? And in the opening thereof we need not deal in worn-out platitudes, but in the almost unused certitudes of the Sacrament. How plentiful they are!

The loss of this privilege of gazing upon the work of a painter was somewhat compensated by a later opportunity of looking into the heart of a Boy Scout. Wesley's rectory, hard by City Road Chapel, London, had been visited and viewed: Visited with interest; viewed with "wonder, love, and praise." A hand-painted portrait of Methodism's patron saint was noticed to be on sale in the study of the man who, unconsciously, "had a church on his hands." The price seemed a bit too demanding, and the portrait was *left* on sale. That last night in London, before sailing home, the portrait came to my mental view and desire. Numerous duties forbade a last-moment return to the Wesley parsonage for the portrait. But the portrait must be secured, if at a sacrifice. The parsonage of City Road Chapel was called by telephone, and after expressing my desire for the portrait, the daughter of the minister informed me, "I'll have one of our Scouts bring it to your hotel." Some of these manly young fellows had been seen in the church choir of that historic Methodist shrine on the previous Sabbath. Later I was to meet one in person, and he was to teach me—something about the Communion.

Before many moments had passed a manly little fellow, about the age of fourteen, walked into my down-town hotel and addressed me in typical English style and brogue. I sat at his feet and learned. After passing a bit of pleasant time with him, I offered to pay him for his services. "You owe me nothing, sir," was his reply. But I insisted, "I owe you something for your trouble and time," and reached for my pocketbook. Again came the answer, "No, sir, you do not owe me anything. I'm a Boy Scout, and a Scout accepts no remuneration for his services of kindness." Ah, that placed a different light on the transaction. I was sorry that it was not my privilege to reward him, but insisted by saying, "Well, if that be the case, let's go to the drug store and get some ice cream." The lad dropped his head, waited for a moment, then said, *"That would be accepting something,* wouldn't it?" "Yes," I replied, "it *would.*" How close I had unconsciously gotten to that lad's Scout oath! How closely I came to making him break his oath! It was my ignorance, and his knowledge. Then, in vain, came my words, "Well, you'll allow me to pay your car fare, won't you? How much is that?" "Tuppence," was the reply. Less than a nickel was all he would accept for his expense money. I walked with him, and reluctantly bade him good-by.

Yes, "that would be accepting something"! I wonder if I am as faithful in accepting the "oath" of my ordination vows as an elder in the Church of God, as I administer the Communion upon certain occasions, as this Scout was toward his vows? His code of Scout ethics forbade him to accept any remuneration. My code of honor forbids me to "slur" over the service of the Sacrament, lest some of the sheep who are hungry look up "and are not fed." All that was dear and near, internal and eternal, of the glowing life of the Son of God went into the chalice. To pass these contributions of His stainless, sinless life out and on becomes the task, yea, the challenge, of the Church of this revealing hour; the challenge of the Church of the days yet to burst upon us with their compelling appeals.

V

THE FAMILY OF CHRIST

DR. ALBERT BELDEN voices his triumphant hope of Christendom's unity in these words, "Her unity is still unachieved, but never was the Church more stricken in conscience concerning her disunity than to-day." There is assuredly a desire for some type of Church union being breathed through the Christian world to-day. If, and when, this dream comes true, and our prayers are heard, one of the most delicate problems to be wrestled with will be the problem of the administration of the Lord's Supper, and of the reception of the same. In this glow and blast of union unction whither are we bound with regard to the Communion?

Whatever divisions there may be to-day in Christendom were not made by God. They were fashioned by the cunning hand of man. We have ascended the spiritual heights when we have declared with Paul, "For ye have not received the spirit of bondage again to fear; but ye have received the Spirit of adoption, whereby we cry, Abba, Father. The Spirit itself beareth witness with our spirit, that we are the children of God; and if children, then heirs." If God be our Father, we are his children. We be brothers! We belong to the same family.

> "We are not divided,
> All one body we,
> One in hope and doctrine,
> One in charity."

If this be not the present realization of Christendom, it most certainly is its prayer. Toward its realization Christianity presses on.

There was an abundance of unity in the Lausanne Conference, but some of the delegates called a halt when the Communion was spread and presented. Dr. Peter Ainslie recently said, in speaking of this Conference: "In 1927 the intercommunion service was dodged, but it will not be dodged again. There is not a greater instance of tomfoolery in religion than the sectarian notion that certain Christians cannot partake of the Lord's Supper with certain other Christians because some Christians have access to a supply of canned grace hermetically sealed in the days of the apostles from all followers of Jesus except those who are episcopally ordained. That may do in the field of patents and copyrights, but to associate it with Jesus is the rankest kind of sectarianism." This merely expresses the free opinion of some of the leaders in Christian thought and polity to-day. Others are equally as free in saying that the amount of water used in one's Christian baptism need not determine who shall administer or receive the Sacrament. Christ must be more concerned about the purity of one's heart, and the purpose of one's soul, than about the volume of water used in a certain Sacrament of the Church.

A high point was reached in a former pastorate with some of my "brothers of the cloth." A union service was conducted in the Presbyterian Church, to which people of four, five, or six denominations came. A Methodist layman delivered the sermon. A Methodist minister read the order for the administration of the Lord's Supper from a Methodist Discipline, and then passed the elements to the several ministers in the pulpit, after which Elders, Deacons, and Stewards passed the Sacrament to the people as they sat in the pews. A year later a minister of the Disciples Church preached from the Methodist pulpit. A Presbyterian minister, reading the Presbyterian form for the administration of the elements, invited the people of the union

service forward to a Methodist altar to partake of the
tokens of love and thoughtfulness which Christ left his disciples.   Rarely, if ever, have I seen people more inwardly
moved.   They felt as though they were really brothers together in Christ; that they belonged to God's family, and
were eating at the family table.   I have always had the
consolation that Christ must have looked on with eyes of
approval.

In these days of rush and hurry the family table in
many homes has been discarded for want of use.   The
breakfast-nook is used; it is used in accord with the time
the members of the family arise and partake of the morning meal.   The father takes lunch down town, and the
children eat their noonday meal at the high school cafete-
ria.   Unless evening engagements prevent, the family may
have the chance of getting together for the evening meal.
No sweeter experience can ever be recalled by man to-day
than the happy times when gathered around the family
table, with father at the head of the table, mother at the
foot, and the children scattered in between.   Christ was the
"Host at every meal."   God not only paused in Creation's
sunrise to make families, but he paused, and paused once
again, in order that he might make provisions whereby it
would be possible for there to be a family of God on earth.
Redemption's plan was made in Eden.   It met its fruition
on Golgotha.   And, in between and ever since, man, accepting the simple terms of redemption, has become a member
of the family of God.   God's heart became tender—it must
have fluttered a bit—when he made families in his own
image.

The Supper scene was a family scene.   Note the record.
The Father, with a mother's heart, was there with his
children.   The Supper was eaten in a selected house, not
in a synagogue.   Not in a cathedral, with spire piercing
the night's blackness.   Not in a million-dollar church, with

polished mahogany altars. It was not administered by priests in flowing garments, nor by richly clad clergymen. Man has added these trappings. In some of our additions we have left the original. The Christ was the One in charge. His garments were not expensive, neither were they conspicuous. Simplicity characterized his dress. Simplicity crowned his words. The additions in words have been made by man. It was a select group of people who partook of the first Supper. The select in heart continue the practice. He broke the bread and poured the wine "with my disciples," after their faithful hands had prepared it. I have often wondered if Judas was one of the communion stewards. He who acts in this capacity has a holy task. Communion stewards are usually some of Christ's most faithful. It was eventide when he "sat down with the twelve." There were no invited guests that night. He had previously eaten with his disciples midst the throngs, despite the fact that some of the number would "send them away." His words that night were to be too intimate, too personal, too soulful for the ears of the average passer-by or invited guest to hear. That was the night in which the Master withheld very little from his own.

It was an interesting conversation in which they engaged. Yet it was sad. The Master was going away. Never more on earth would He eat that Supper with them. His own heart was sad, and thus were the hearts of the disciples saddened. This was always the case. When he was glad, they were glad. When he was troubled, they were troubled. It was a pathetic scene. The children of the Father were perplexed and worried. It was a dark scene, for it was night. Yet there was a Star in the sky, and its rays penetrated the blackness of that Jerusalem night. That Star had arisen in Bethlehem of Judæa only a few years previously. It had followed him wherever he had gone. It had watched over him wherever he had slept, whether in the home of Lazarus or on the mountain side from which he had come to brush the dew-drops from his locks and speak "Peace, be still" to the waves, thus comforting the distressed disciples. The rays of the Star had shone, and their invitation had led a be-nighted people from the confines of their own darkened spaces to the glow of the Sun of righteousness; yea, to the glory of the Son of God. And there was hope in that family scene, for his request, that he be not forgotten, was certain to be carried out by the people who dare to follow in His footprints.

I am speaking of the conversation around the supper table that night. Ah! these family conversations! What do they mean? Where do they get us? A home can come nearer being a heaven on earth than any place of which we know. Again, a home can come nearer being a hell on earth than any place in our knowledge. Many homes are only houses, with a roof for a covering. Eddie Guest was right when he said, "It takes a heap o' livin' in a house to make it home." I pause to say it, but there was friction in the upper room at that last meal. Jesus drew back from friction. He plunged forward in a holy desire to eliminate it. But friction arose within the group: not friction toward one another. That type of friction had arisen previously as to who should occupy the most impor-tant place in the kingdom. The friction was toward Christ. He did not cause it to arise. He knew it was compelled to present its ugly fangs. Said he, "One of you shall betray me." That thought was the most remote within the minds of—at least—eleven of his inner group. But the record says, "Every one of them" began to ask him if he were the one who was to do the ugly, black deed. Here is hypocrisy at its height. Judas, the soon-to-be betrayer, joined in the shout, "Is it I?" Judas knew.

Christ did not cause him to become a betrayer; he only permitted it. Christ permits things which are within our power to change, if we are of such a mind and purpose. Judas was not of the purpose to change his plans.

But the friction was soon conspicuous for its absence. Its dismissal was at its own hand. Judas went out to be the pitiful, "miserable sneak." The Sacrament cannot, and will not, progress in its spiritual application and results with friction abiding at sacramental altars. God forbid that I should manifest the attitude of condemnation of my brother who does not think as I! I would not relish his condemnation were he to condemn me for not thinking as he. Some of my brothers administer the Sacrament once a week. They have good Scripture for their actions. When George Whitefield began to carry out his heart-longing for God, and for more of God, he made some very rigid rules for his own spiritual development. He began to fast every Wednesday and Friday, and to partake of the Sacrament every Sunday. Other Christian communions have different stated times in which the Sacrament shall be administered. In the Church of my nativity it was my custom to partake of the Sacrament on the first Sunday of the month. In my own ministry the Sacrament is administered on the first Sunday of every other month, with special communions on special days in addition. My purpose for selecting these days of the calendar year is for the reason that my observation has led me to conclude that too frequent communions have seemed, at least from observation, to make the Communion too common. Upon these special occasions of the year, the best I have—little as it is—is thrown into the service, that it may be one of the high peaks of the Church year. The observations of such a program are that the results have been, at least, encouraging. At times there have been members of the Church family who were shut-ins who could not make their way to the sanctuary; and with gladness of heart and purity of purpose the elements have been taken to their bedsides, where another communion table was sacredly erected. Especially have I found this service effective on the opening day of the Lenten season. Christ is not particularly interested in dates or the trappings of man, but he must surely be interested in the condition of the hearts of his children.

Christendom is chock-full of denominations. But does Jesus approve of the tidal waves of denominationalism? We proudly say, "One faith, one Lord, one baptism," and at the same time new denominations are being created, while others are uniting. His high priestly prayer was voiced in favor of himself, his disciples, and "for them which shall believe on me." He prayed for the joy, preservation, and sanctification of his disciples. Then he seemed to hasten on to pray for the believers since his day, petitioning that "they may all be one." This petition he repeats. And later he says, "That they may be made *perfect* in *one*." There was unity at Pentecost. The followers of Christ were all with "one accord." That is why Pentecost came. Had there been a lack of unity, the Holy Spirit would have delayed his coming until harmony and unity had been attained.

Without further comment, the question is asked: "What does Christ think of our divisions, of our varied methods of administration of the Communion, of our altars built against altars? What does he think of these creations of man in the light of his high priestly prayer, and in the revealing, searching light of the truth of Pentecost? Hasn't the day already dawned when Christians shall begin to live together as brothers? We have said in loud tones, "We be brothers"; but have our actions been as manifest as our words? Has not the day about arrived when we shall be willing to make some concessions, if necessary—

and it shall be necessary—to make some additions—to make some subtractions in order that Christendom shall be more of a union, more of a united force, more of "one great army we"? A statement, almost trite, but so true, but the motto of one of the Southern Commonwealths proclaims, "United we stand, divided we fall."

To whom does the Sacrament of the Lord's Supper belong? It is the possession of true Christendom! But Christendom possesses her several different and separate denominations, each believing that their own method, perhaps, of presenting the truths of Christ are better than, or at least as good as, any other branch of Christendom. Each of the denominations harps back to history. Our Roman Catholic brethren claim Peter as the first Pope. They claim that his sacred dust is buried beneath Michelangelo's great dome in St. Peter's, Rome. Silently I stood in that great, impressive church of Christian worship. I saw the devotees of that faith come in streams into the impressive entrance, cross themselves, dip their fingers in the "holy water," and humbly approach the life-size bronze statue of St. Peter, which stands hard by the high altar. No mother ever caressed the child of her bosom more tenderly than some of those Catholic devotees kiss the large toe of the Apostle Peter. The toe has been kissed so often by the lips, and rubbed so often by the fingers of these local and world pilgrims of this faith, that it is perceptibly wearing away. Think of human lips and fingers wearing away bronze! In the same city under the high altar of Saint-Paul's-without-the-Walls rests, what is reputed to be, the mortal remains of the great Apostle to the Gentiles. This great Church, with all her trappings and wrappings, her ceremonies, feasts, and fasts, places a claim upon the proper and religiously legitimate manner of presenting and receiving the Sacrament.

Protestantism, in all her many claims and divisions, some

branches dating their orgin back to John the Baptizer; others dating their beginning at Pentecost; others with Wesley in England—Protestantism invites her devotees to remember the Crucified in his Last Supper. Christendom administers and receives the broken and spilt tokens of his life and death, but these are received at different altars. Our theological beliefs and interpretations are the cause of the erection of these separate altars. Thanks be to God, these partitions are being broken down. Our children and grandchildren shall witness greater evidences of the truth of united Christendom communing at united altars than do we of this day.

I love my Church and am devoted to its ministry. But I refuse to administer the Sacrament *as a Methodist, as a denominationalist,* or *as a creedalist.* I joyfully present the elements *as a Christian,* "washed in the blood of the Lamb." Denominations are too small at the Communion chancel. Creeds are too narrow at the sacred Table. Only Christianity—in all its world scope and interpretation— will suffice. This is Christianity's breadth. It is its depth. The Communion is not the possession of denominations; it is the possession of Christianity. It is not to be claimed by the creeds; but it is to be received by Christians. The only sense in which it may rightly belong to creedalism is that when it is applied to the creed of Christ.

Senator Edward Ward Carmack, a son of the Southland, once rose in an impromptu moment upon the floor of the United States Senate and made his immortal "pledge to the South." In my youth, as I endeavored to orate in the literary society, that speech thrilled me. It captivated me. It made my blood boil. Since then I have applied some of its words to my Church. What Senator Carmack said of the South, I say of my Church, the Church of my fathers, and the Church of my choice: "I was born of her womb; I was nurtured at her breast, and when my last hour shall come, I pray God that I may be pillowed upon her bosom and rocked in sleep within her encircling arms. To that Church every drop of my blood, every fiber of my being, every pulsation of my heart is consecrated forever." But, if in this crusade throughout the world for Christian fraternalism, united worship, world brotherhood, and the acceptance of the universal creed of Christ, it becomes necessary for my Church to surrender any precious "idol of Methodism" in order for Christian union to be attained around the festal board of the Church of God on earth, and that Christ's children may really become in profession and possession members of the family of God, I am ready, and I prophesy that Methodism is ready. God grant that Christendom may hasten this glorious day! And he is already serving to answer that prayer of the yearning soul.

VI

LIFE'S TAPESTRY

LIFE'S EXPERIENCES produce biographies. Biographies develop into histories of the human race. Histories are but the woven tapestries of individual lives as they are connected with the intimate affairs and details of a nation's progress. It is of the *individual* rather than of the *nation* of whom we are thinking and of whom we write. The pleasures and adversities of life have a way of blending together until they form a tapestry—a tapestry of beauty.

Jesus had been talking with his disciples of the experiences which were to be his. He informed them that he must "suffer many things"; that he would be "rejected of the elders," and that he would be "slain," but the resurrection would follow as certainly as sunrise follows sunset. Then he turned and said to them, "If any man will come after me, let him deny himself, take up his cross daily, and follow me." They *grasped* at the opportunity of following him, but they *gasped* at the thought of denying themselves, and were confounded at the teaching of daily cross-bearing. Jesus did not stop when he discerned their reactions to his statement, and proceeded to say, "Whosoever will save his life, shall lose it; but whosoever will lose his life for my sake, the same shall find it." That was so reactionary, so different, so peculiar—yea, it was so difficult. The reactions of modern Christians in America are strikingly similar to those of the first Christians in Galilee.

In such a teaching there is the Christian's secret of a happy life. The happiest people are those who lose themselves. A visit to a rayon factory proved illuminating when it was shown that through a mixture of waste cotton with a solution of copper sulphate a silky, fine, delicate substance of rayon silk was secured. The cotton, which was declared "waste," was rescued and placed with chemicals in order that it might lose itself, that it might lose its identity, in order for it to become a product of finer texture, more costly, and more salable. It gained by losing. Lost sinful identities of self, selfishness, and waste always result in gained personalities through Christ. The mission of our Lord was to save the *loss,* the *lost,* and the *last.* Man must go by the route of losing himself. This is the way of gain, according to the logic of Jesus.

The well-developed Christian is the one who fellowships with sorrow and clasps the hand of joy. He gives himself. A safe and sheltered existence makes for a saddened life. A life empty of grief, care, and a reasonable amount of trouble will result in a saddened life. Longfellow said:

> "Into each life some rain must fall,
> Some days must be dark and dreary."

That does not mean that we are to carry with us our umbrellas lest some of the rain of hardship fall upon our untroubled heads. The tragedy of many a life is that it has been withheld. If the flowers withheld their perfume, from whence would come fragrance? If the birds withheld their songs, from whence would come the initial omens of bursting, gladsome spring? If the babe withheld its infant smile, from whence could we secure a true portrait of the Creator? If the mother withheld her life, her blood, her care, her affection, her strength from the child of her bosom, from whence would we eventually secure adulthood? If man refrains from the experience of losing himself, how can he ever hope to find himself? Finding by losing is the only route. Gains by losses! That was Jesus' way of teaching.

Tapestry-making was found in early times in places so far apart as Peru, Egypt, and China. To-day tapestries are made by power looms and by hand. In the power loom the exact repetition of design follows as naturally as the multiplication of copies of a printed book, while there is no more reason why tapestries should be alike than why paintings should be alike. Handmade tapestries are all different. The trained eye readily observes the difference, just as the trained eye of the artist quickly discerns the points and shades of difference in a painting. God did not make us machines, as the mechanistic psychologists argue. He made us individuals, with the power to produce our own pattern; with the gift of weaving, by hand, our own tapestry. The Creator must have thought a million years and more before he decided to make man with the freedom of choice. His decision has proven the wisdom of the Creator. Each of these personally woven tapestries is decidedly different, because the choice of individuals is different. Handmade tapestries are more tedious than those which are machine-made. They are more costly. Every life produces a handmade tapestry. Almost incredible pains are taken to see that material and workmanship are the best. The material and workmanship which constitute the weaving of life's tapestry must be the best, if the product is to be of the highest quality. It costs. It costs big. "Whosoever will save his life, shall lose it."

In the case of a set of tapestries woven at Brussels to commemorate the conquest of Tunis by the Emperor Charles V there were stipulations controlling the kind of thread to be used and the proportion of metal thread to wool and silk. The Emperor provided the gold and silk threads, and his agent spent more than two years at Granada supervising the preparation and dyeing of the silk. Eighty-four weavers were to be continually employed on the twelve panels, and a commission was appointed to superintend the work. Strict regulations were made, and penalties for the infringement upon these regulations were severe. Distinguished artists were engaged to watch the process of the work. If these be the circumstances under which one of the great sets of tapestries of the world were made, what must be the circumstances under which the tapestries of the lives of God's children are woven? The trained eye of the Artist is focused upon the workmanship. Certain portions have been furnished by Him, and his children must furnish their part as they work under the direction of his sympathetic hand.

Tapestries are costly, not only on account of being hand-woven, but due to the assembling of various colors. All experiences of life are necessary to produce the colors in a spiritual masterpiece. Man must have the bitter and the sweet. A tapestry of one color is not desired by the purchaser. The tragedy about life is that *so many lives are of one color*. They are so changeless. They possess no novelty, no surprise, because their experiences have been on the level of spiritual inactivity. Their spiritual explorations have been few. Their sacrifices have been scarce. Their tears have been infrequent. Their crosses—if any at all—have been light—most too light to discern their presence. They have lived the withheld life. It has been sheltered—sheltered from the rains of sadness, sheltered from the sun of sorrow, protected from the night of agony, sheltered from the storms of life's short day.

The trained eye of a passenger on a New England train noticed that the birches of the New Hampshire woods had been bent: those white birches which, when storms do not come, stand slender, shining, and straight—"which stand out against the sturdier tree companions, against the dark fir and pine and hemlock like the ideal type of feminine beauty." "Terrible ice storms we had here last winter," commented the congenial conductor, as the train sped on its way. "Those trees will never stand straight again," he said. And that reminds me of what Robert Frost had seen and said:

> "When I see birches bent to left and right
> Across the lines of straighter, darker trees,
> I like to think some boy's been swinging them.
> But swinging doesn't bend them down to stay.
> *Ice-storms do that.*"

But who wants an "ice-storm"? Who wants denial? Who wants to lose? When I stand in my pulpit and see before me the wrinkled face, with the clear eye and the hopeful brow, I am led to know that "ice-storms" have come upon such souls, but the immortal look is visible to all who have eyes to see. "Ice-storms" for the sake of Him who had the storms of sinful man beat upon Him, but which did not change the set of His sails! These "ice-storms" go into the perfection of life's tapestry.

Observation, and conversation with those who have gone over much of life's way, lead us to believe that the happiest people are not the best-protected people. The protected life is the anemic life. It is so bloodless. It is so pitifully pale and peaked. In the record of Paul's missionary experiences, these words stand out in holy boldness and flaming challenge, "We must through much tribulation enter the kingdom." I fear—I greatly fear—that the modern Church member shies off from that teaching. "Tribulation" has little — too little — appeal to modern Christians. "Every stormy wind that blows" has little part in our vocabulary, and a lesser part in our Christian experience. Yet, the color gained in the vale of tribulation is necessary for the weaving, not by loom, but by hand, of the tapestries of our spiritual experiences.

> "Must I be carried to the skies
> On flowery beds of ease,
> While others fought to win the prize,
> And sailed through bloody seas?"

Isaac Watts did not stop with that interrogation, placed in rhythm and tune, but answered in a later verse:

"Sure I must fight, if I would reign;
Increase my courage, Lord;
I'll *bear the toil, endure the pain,*
Supported by thy word."

It was George Watts, English sculptor and painter, who looked at life, and life's future, through the spectacles of a restful and gleaming hope, in one of his subject pictures, in which he represents "Sic Transit," showing a corpse, with the famous inscription, "What I spent, I had; what I saved, I lost; what I gave, I have." Losing by saving! Having by giving! That is the secret.

Two girls grew up together. They had been schoolgirl companions, and when middle life came on they still possessed a schoolgirl intimacy. One of the women had married. She had become a mother. Her husband went to war, and died a soldier's death. Her son was taken later in the influenza epidemic. She had known the possession of wealth, but that too had been swept from her grasp, and now she has taken a position in the great world of business. The other woman, her dear friend, had not married, and had not borne. She had been privileged to live in a large white house, surrounded by a beautiful garden. Her hair had not faded like the hair of her friend's. Her face was not wrinkled. But the face of her friend was gradually taking on the wrinkles of hardship. She had lived a life which was peaceful and uneventful. Her life had been safe and sheltered—and unattached from the world. She had no spark in her eyes, no conversation, and no mirth. Her friend who had lost had also loved. The life of the second woman was empty of grief, and hence empty of fulfillment. Her "milestones had not been dewed with tears." The first woman knew the dark hour and its gripping interpretation—its silent, truthful voice. She had lost and won. She had given and gained. She was the more interesting and the happier of the two. Her life had been sadder, but it dared to be gladder. She had lived the poured-out life. She dared not do otherwise. Can the Church dare do otherwise — to take any other course of procedure? If Dr. H. King was right when he said, "Then measure thy life by loss instead of gain, not by the wine drunk, but by the wine poured forth," we dare not attempt to produce any other type and pattern of Christian experience than the poured-out life.

It has been said truthfully that some painters have, in an endeavor to secure a certain shading for the picture upon which they have been working, pierced their veins, and, dipping the brush in their own blood, secured a perfection of color, one which brought out the richest mixture of art. Such paintings will not fade. This is the reason why Jesus' life will not, and cannot, fade. His life's blood is in the picture. The blood which coursed through his veins was his life, his strength. When he gave it, he gave himself. When he lost it, he lost himself. This is the explanation of the Cross. This is the secret of the Sacrament. Jesus not only transformed the Cross, but the Cross transformed Jesus. It was to him the cup of his sacrifice. The transaction there caused the stream of life-giving power and healing influence to flow down the side of a world in need. Hence we sing, with William Cowper:

> "There is a fountain filled with blood,
> Drawn from Immanuel's veins;
> And sinners, plunged beneath that flood,
> Lose all their guilty stains."

This is why we read again with zest and hope, "For God so loved the world THAT HE GAVE." Wondrous Gift! Gift Divine! When man fails to give, he ceases to live. He loses by retention, he becomes humble by condescension, he gains by presentation. "Present your bodies a living sacrifice" are the Apostle's words in this regard. Dr. E. Stanley Jones says, "Souls wither under self-saving." Withered souls are the result of withheld lives. Shriveled souls are the result of self-saving. To lose ourselves we must loose ourselves. Loosened from the ties that bind us! Too firmly are we "chained to our idols." We are become modern Ephraims!—chained, and thus maimed. Chained by our own hands! Maimed by our own practices!

The mingling of the varied experiences of the brief years in which our Saviour lived on earth caused the production of a marvelous piece of tapestry. He was subjected to every temptation in the physical form. In our endeavor to emphasize the divinity of our Lord, we have overlooked to a large measure his humanity. This explains why so much of modern theology has been written with the humanity of Jesus in the foreground. His divinity is earth's greatest miracle, in which I reverently believe. Is not his humanity a miracle also? The combination of the two is almost beyond our comprehension, but not beyond our faith. No, man has not been able to explain the divine birth. But has he been able to explain the human birth? Jesus' humanity was subjected to all experiences. He faced the scorn as well as the praise. He experienced the storm and reveled in the calm. He drank the bitter and the sweet, was covered by the gloom, and rejoiced in the bloom—the bloom of hope and a Voice which led on. He walked midst darkness, and toiled in the light. He knew the chill of hatred, and the warmth of devotion. He knew the attitude of cool hearts, cold hearts, and hot hearts. He read the thermometer of men's lives most accurately. He knew what it was to receive the extremes of affection and the superlatives of anger and hate. He received a poured-out affection, and then an avalanche of persecutions. He knew the haunts of the sinful, and the shrines of the saints. He made acquaintance with the walk of the lowly, and received the sneers of the haughty. He experienced loss that he might bear a cross. What a tapestry was our Lord's! And if we are to "share" the "fellowship of his sufferings," we must bear his Cross. His body was broken that it might be a token. The fruitage of his life was crushed that the essence of his love might be drunk. He excelled in living the poured-out life. He bids us, even as he did the fishermen, to "follow me." There was a lift in his life in order that there might be a Gift in his life. He was lifted up. He had to go down in submission before he could be raised in transformation. Wondrous Example! The aroma of his life crowds the nostrils of the world. The perfume of his life can be sensed in every clime.

How difficult it is to bury some people! The "six feet of dirt" fails to cover them. It covers their fading body, but it fails to cover the real soul of the deceased. "Their works do follow them." The aroma of their lives and the perfume of their Christian influence live on. There is a simple but lasting lesson in the manufacture of perfume. The perfumes which are sold in corner drug stores come from various sources, such as flowers, leaves, stems, barks, woods, roots, fruits, seeds, and gums. Such flowers as the carnation, cassia, clove, hyacinth, heliotrope, mimosa, jasmine, jonquil, orange blossom, rose, violet, and the ylang-ylang are used in perfume manufacture. The separation of the natural odoriferous material from the plant or flower is a difficult matter. Some methods are most expensive. Producers of perfumes extract what is called "absolute flower oil." This is the most expensive type of perfumery. In the raw material, especially in the case of the jasmine, the product is worth from fifteen dollars to thirty dollars an ounce, according to the flower crop. The quantity of this flower used per annum for oil, or other processes, has for many years exceeded 1,300 tons, while in the case of orange blossoms it is even 2,000 tons. I am convinced that the "absolute flower oil" extracted from the lives of God's elect is that aroma which is not buried when the loved one is put away by kind hands in the best that money can buy.

There used to live down in Mississippi a godly woman. Her devoted companion, a man successful in his life's work, was called by death in the prime of his life. The widowed mother gathered her brood around her and started out life's activities again. She did not house herself in, nor cover herself with the outward crêpe of eternal mourning. She busied herself about the rearing of her children, and the service of her neighbors, always filling her place in her church, to which she was most faithfully consecrated. She knew and loved her Bible. Its pages were like "streams in the desert" to her. The great poets were her daily companions. She reveled in reading all good works. Travel fell to her lot. God placed within her crystal soul a happy heart. She was especially gifted in the art of saying good things about other people. As she was rounding out her fourscore years the Master stepped down and said, "Come with me." And she, who believed so profoundly with Browning,

> "Grow old along with me,
> The best is yet to be,
> The last of life for which the first was made,"

suffered rather severely for several weeks. But, with her beloved Tennyson, she "put out to sea" with a smile. "She is not gone, she is just away." Her life cannot be buried. It lives on. Her tapestry was one of varied hues, akin to the diversified lots which were hers. We are told that the longer a perfume will remain fragrant after application to a handkerchief or a garment, the more popular it be-

comes, on account of its *enduring* nature. The aroma of
the life of this good woman, who had the smile of eternity
upon her forehead, possessed an enduring nature and an
abiding influence after the application of her life to the
garments of those who rise up to-day "to call her blessed."

Helen Keller has made a contribution to life because of
her compelled sacrifice. It is difficult to receive the aroma
of some flowers until they are crushed. It is said that the
sweetest of perfumes comes from a flower which blooms
at night. Miss Keller's life was crushed; therefore it sent
out an aroma. As I write these words the mother who
bore me, together with nine other children, is approaching
her seventy-sixth birthday. One of her choice diversions
has been the making of pretty, useful, dainty things by her
ever-busy maternal hands. Some of these creations of
her hands are always sent to her children at Christmas
time. They are a part of "the warp and woof of her life,"
and are cherished with delight. Yet the contributions of
her soul are cherished more dearly than these. Her life
has been sweetened through sorrow. Her strength has in-
creased through sacrifice. Her service has glowed through
its constant multiplication. Her face has been softened
by the hand of Time, and her eyes have been made brighter
by the glow of eternity which has rested in them since
the days of early married life, when, as a young married
couple, she and my father gave themselves into the keeping
of God's guiding hands. As I have expressed my thanks
to various people for the contributions to my life of worth-
whileness, upon a recent day I looked into the calm, ex-
pressive face of the pastor who, in his early ministry, led
my parents to God, and said, "I thank you." Such paren-
tal influence shall never fade. It is of eternal endurance.
I count this my greatest earthly heritage. It is better than
gold, "yea, than fine gold." With Margaret Sangster,

"I weave upon my tapestry,
  With colors dark and fair;
Some represent a lovely dream,
  Some colors are a prayer!
Some colors stand for lonely days,
  Some stand for happiness,
Some are as somber as a storm,
  Some soft as a caress.

I weave upon my tapestry,
  I make a brave design—
And what I like about it, best,
  Is that it's wholly *mine!*
And yet it is not mine alone,
  Ah, that I understand!
For as I weave my tapestry,
  God's finger guides my hand."

VII

REPENTANCE IN THE LIGHT OF THE SACRAMENT

RETURNING FROM THE SOUTH POLE, Admiral Richard Byrd said, "We have explored everything except our consciences." The interesting thing about this statement is not its frank truthfulness, but the fact that a scientific explorer, an aviator, said it. But the pendulum among the conservatives and among the moderns is swinging back toward the application of the gospel to the personal—the conscience—the individual approach. This drift is to be welcomed. It is to be cultivated. It is to be received with hopeful spirits. It is to be anchored within our own thought life, and within the harbors of our own sympathetic meditations.

One of the most theologically progressive ministers of our land recently said: "What damns the Church of our generation more than any other defect is its inability, or unwillingness, to preach an adequate gospel of repentance." The modern Church has shied off from the gospel of repentance. Such a gospel, in these modern, illumined days, has been called ancient. The Church has had an attitude that it has gone beyond that stage where it was wise, or necessary, to preach such a gospel. In so doing, she has been the loser. She has been found wanting. When the Church ceases this insistence, religion becomes human, it is lost. When it becomes human, it is without an anchor. "The insistence of religion upon repentance is the measure of its divinity." When religion loses its repentance, it loses its divinity. When it loses its divinity, it loses itself. When it loses itself, it becomes lost to every one else. It isn't worth finding. The search is too hopeless and too expensive.

The truest of the prophets made contrition the basis of admission into the religious fold. They called upon the people to possess contrite hearts. The Pslamist, in his prayer for the remission of his own sins, exclaimed, "The sacrifices of God are a broken spirit: a broken and a contrite heart . . . thou wilt not despise." But a great amount of preaching of contrition has ceased to be. And herein, have we not lost rather than gained? The modern age has had little to say in regard to "sackcloth and ashes." The repentant Church approaches the Sacrament in sackcloth and ashes, while the non-repentant Church makes its approach in broadcloth and sashes. The whole matter of repentance and contrition has its background in the presence of sin. But "some moderns choose to hope for the day when men will be delivered from the sense of sin." This statement is doubly interesting and impressive when we read it as coming from the lips of one of the most outstanding "moderns." Thank God, we may be delivered from sin, through Christ's intervention; but pity the Church when we are ever—if ever—delivered from the *sense* of sin. "Sin lieth at the door" in Eden. It lieth at my door in America. "My sin is ever before me," with David. The sense of its presence, its blackness, hovers round about *my* study. It steps into my parish. The sense of sin is the keen consciousness of its presence and its power— the consciousness of its binding, blinding, grinding nature! Sin still bites "like a serpent." No one of such pulpit fame and eloquence sensed the presence and power of sin, in its ravaging work and venomous effects, any more powerfully than the sainted Dr. John Henry Jowett. He placed his impressions of sin in this mold:

Sin is a blasting presence, and every fine power shrinks and withers in the destructive heat. Every spiritual delicacy succumbs to its malignant touch. I suppose that Scripture has drawn upon every sense for analogies in which to express the ravages of sin in the region of perception. Sin impairs the sight and works toward blindness. Sin benumbs the hearing and tends to make men deaf. Sin perverts the taste, causing men to confound the sweet with the bitter, and the bitter with the sweet. Sin hardens the touch, and eventually renders a man "past feeling." . . . Sin blocks and chokes the fine senses of the spirit; by sin we are desensitized, rendered imperceptive, and the range of our correspondence is diminished. Sin creates callosity. It hoofs the spirit, and so reduces the area of our exposure to pain.

Repentance is God's way of getting rid of sin. It has been his only method. Prayer is man's way of retaining the consciousness of the sense of sin. Repentance runs like a glossy, silken thread throughout the New Testament. John the Baptizer came "preaching, saying, Repent ye." His announcement of his plans for baptism came in these terse and impressive words, "I baptize you with water *unto repentance.*" With John, there was no occurrence of baptism unless it was preceded by repentance. John's Successor "began to preach, Repent." He began where John left off. The foregleams of the mantle of Christ fell upon the Jordan preacher. The afterglow of the mantle of John rested upon the youthful shoulders of the Nazareth Minister. They preached the same gospel of "repentance unto salvation." When the Nazarene sent out the men of the Inner Circle, they took up the refrain, "And they went out, and preached that men should repent." They announced with their Master, "Except ye repent, ye shall all . . . perish."

Where in all the world of sacred literature is there to be found a more tender portrayal of fatherly love than in the great parable of a son who went away from home, perhaps prematurely, and later came back? Where can we discover a portrait of paternal affection and filial regret comparable with the lad who came back under the hovering confines of a father's rooftree? The record of the going and the return of the Prodigal Son is not only a literary masterpiece, but it is a perfect tapestry of God's goodness; a divine mosaic of an undying love, ever abiding within the Father's house. Couched within the heart of it all are these words, "Father, I have sinned . . . and am no more worthy to be called thy son." There is the perfection of repentance—that repentance which was born when the lonesome, starved, homesick lad breathed within the nobleness and hope of a youthful soul and said, "I will arise and go to my father." As far as he was concerned, the repentance had already occurred. The words spoken at the meeting of himself and his father were only a repetition of his thoughts and conclusions down by the swine pen of his employer. It is almost as interesting to note the father's actions as the actions of the lad. His father did not say "I forgive you" in words, but his actions were more impressive than any words which his lips might have paused to frame at that moment. He was too full for utterance. I have seen my noble father too full for speech, and in that sight I can better see and understand the prodigal's father. The father turned immediately and began to command that the garments and trinkets which would signify and certify forgiveness be brought at once. The "best robe," the "ring," the "shoes," the banquet of undying affection were brought and hastily prepared. Ere that banquet was eaten it was announced throughout that land over what aërials they might have possessed, "My son was dead, and is alive again; he was lost, and is found." But this tapestry of love would never have been woven, this mosaic of affection would never have been completed, this rhapsody of exultant praise would never have been experienced unless—unless—there had been within the procedure a genuine experience of repentance upon the part of the sinner in the parable.

An Apocalyptic writer also preaches the gospel of repentance. It is to that Church which had been so prominent among the Churches of Asia, but which had left its first love, that the writer sings out and says, "Remember from whence thou art fallen, and repent." To at least two other Churches of the "Asiatic Conference" the message of repentance was broadcast. Their members had been guilty of sin. Modern writers, in an increasing stream, are saying: "Until we have discovered the sense of sin, there is little hope for a final reconciliation with God the Father. The prodigals of life must be reminded that there is a Father." There is no reconciliation, no repentance, or need of them, without first there is sin, and a consciousness of it within us. Repentances, reconciliations, "upheavals" must occur. Dr. Bucke, in his "Cosmic Consciousness," gives one thousand pages to prove that all great geniuses who have affected the trend of human events have experienced a sudden upheaval, a regeneration. Leading psychologists of the type of James, McDougal, and Coe are agreed on the fact of the necessity of these epochal experiences within the lives of people which turn the slant of their sails.

Repentance is only a condition of salvation and not its meritorious ground. The motives of repentance are chiefly found in the goodness of God, in Divine love, in the pleading desire to have sinners saved, in the inevitable consequences of sin, in the universal demand of the gospel, and in the hope of spiritual life and membership in the kingdom of heaven. The first four Beatitudes form a heavenly ladder by which penitent souls pass from the dominion of Satan into the Kingdom of God. A consciousness of spiritual poverty dethroning pride, a sense of personal unworthiness producing grief, a willingness to surrender to

God in genuine humility, and a strong spiritual desire developing into hunger and thirst enter into the experience of one who wholly abandons sin and heartily turns to Him who grants repentance unto life. Such experiences as these are found in the said Beatitudes.

When I take the Ritual in hand and read "The Order for the Administration of the Lord's Supper," there is a trumpet call to the altar of repentance from beginning to end. In the first sentence of the invitation the communicant is confronted with these words, "Ye that do truly and earnestly repent of your sins." And the communicant who sincerely unites in the "General Confession" repents when saying: "Almighty God . . . we acknowledge and bewail our manifold sins and wickedness . . . which we . . . have committed by thought, word, and deed. . . . We do earnestly repent, and are heartily sorry. . . . The remembrance of them is grievous. . . . Have mercy upon us." Then the minister reads these impressive words: "O Almighty God, our Heavenly Father, who of thy great mercy hast promised forgiveness of sins to all them that with hearty repentance . . . turn to thee." To whom is forgiveness promised? The answer is very explicit, "To all them that *with hearty repentance* . . . turn to thee." Again the Elder prays that "our souls and bodies may be made clean by his death, and washed through his most precious blood." This soul cleansing is made possible through the shedding of Christ's blood; but it must be attached to a repentant heart. When the congregation joins the minister in the Pattern Prayer, this petition is heard with forcefulness, "Forgive us our trespasses as we forgive those who trespass against us." That petition is one which is born out of an experience of repentance. The communicant is sorry. He asks for pardon. He repents.

The elements are passed. The chalice is covered. The linen cloths again cover the communion set, as it rests symbolically upon the "In Remembrance of Me" table. The congregation and minister are kneeling in prayer, and these impressive words are voiced by him who leads in the service: "Grant that . . . we and thy whole Church may obtain remission of our sins." God knows, and man knows, that that "remission" can only come when preceded by an attitude of heart contrition and humble repentance. After this cleansing and partaking an opportunity is given for the truthfully sincere to "present unto thee, O Lord, ourselves, our souls and bodies, to be a . . . sacrifice unto thee." This holy presentation of self and substance is made subsequent to the act of repentance, as the prayer is uttered, "not weighing our merits, but *pardoning* our offenses." And so often there is omitted that part which may be read or sung, in which the worshiper praises the "Lamb of God, Son of the Father, that *takest away the sins of the world.*" "Thou that takest away the sins of the world" is used in three consecutive statements. Surely does the Father take away the sins of the individual, of the world, when those sins are asked to be taken away in a repentant mood and prayer.

In the light of such a service, in the face of such a ritualistic observance, when entered into as humble, hungry, penitent communicants, the Christian arises a "new man." Truly it might be said that the Cross is the heart throb of the Sacrament. Repentance is the tear fall, the teardrop, of the Sacrament. In such an attitude we are brought face to face with a personal religious experience, with religion itself. Modern Methodists must not forget the statement of Bishop Hoss at the Fourth Ecumenical Methodist Conference: "Our stock in trade is our religion. When that goes, we shall be the most poverty-stricken people on the face of the earth, for we have nothing left to fall back upon . . . no long-stretching centuries of history, no moss-covered cathedrals, no monumental volumes of theology, no elaborate ritual of worship. God himself, consciously known, adored, and loved, through Jesus Christ, is our only and our 'everlasting portion.' "

> "Lord, what a change within us one short hour
> Spent in Thy presence will avail to make!
> What heavy burdens from our bosoms take;
> What parched grounds refresh, as with a shower.
> We kneel and all around us seems to lower;
> We rise, and all the distance and the near
> Stands forth in sunny outline, brave and clear!
> We kneel, how weak! we rise, how full of power!"

N. B.—The Ritual referred to in this address and other addresses is that according to the Methodist Episcopal Church, South.

VIII

THE MASTER KEY

If repentance is the door of Communion, consecration is the appeal of Communion. If godly sorrow is the human tear of Communion, Christian dedication is the holy touch of Communion. Not only does consecration follow repentance in the scheme and plan of our Christian theology, but this is the order in our Ritual. It further becomes the practice in our Christian experience.

"Who then is willing to consecrate his service this day unto the Lord?" were the ringing words and the enthusiastic appeal of David as he proceeded to get everything in readiness for the erection of a temple to the Lord, not by his own hands, but by the hands of his son. His appeal met with a wholesome response, for "hundreds and thousands offered willingly." The people brought of their "precious stones," and their choicest possessions, and presented them with a "perfect heart." There was nothing too dear for them to present. David cried out, "In the uprightness of mine heart I have willingly offered all these things." "Then the people rejoiced because they had offered willingly." Rejoicing is always the aftermath of such offerings. The gifts of their possessions resulted in the erection of their temple of worship. If there are to be spiritual temples of worship erected within the lives of the Church membership, there must be the offering—the consecration—of the choicest possessions of our lives to Him who is able to make the "temple of my heart" his own. The approach to Communion altars is the approach to the shrines of personal consecration.

According to the Ritual, which is used every month by many, and with more or less frequency by others, the repentance is made, the Sacrament is passed, and that which remaineth of the consecrated elements is covered "with a fair linen cloth," and this becomes our prayer: "And here we *offer* and *present* unto Thee, O Lord, ourselves, our souls and bodies." In this act and prayer of consecration we are presenting our bodies for service, our souls for worship, and "ourselves," meaning all that we possess, and ever hope to possess, our mental powers, our social contacts, our financial possessions, our substance, to Him "from whom all blessings flow." This is consecration in its entirety. If this consecration were really *practiced* as it is *voiced,* it would revolutionize the Christian Church, solving all her material, financial, and spiritual problems, and would bring in the day for which long the faithful devotees of Christ have prayed. This prayer, fulfilled, would supply an abundant harvest for local Church workers; it would bring into the treasuries of our Lord the means to assist in the propagation of the gospel around the world; it would send youth, with the hope of life's conquest stamped on their foreheads, to the outposts of civilization with the "glad news" of a Redeemer's love. What a Christian Utopia it would bring about! Couched in the Communion are the hope, the dream, the prayer for such a day.

In Old Testament usage the Hebrews, by their acts of consecration, "separated" that which was to be consecrated. It was "devoted" to a certain use, or service. For the installation of a priest into office, as "Thou shalt consecrate Aaron," the word meaning "to fill the hand" was used. Thus, when we consecrate ourselves, we "fill the hand" of the Lord with our life and our life's possessions. The reaction on the part of the one who so consecrates his life is that his hand and his heart are filled. In the New Testament usage that which was consecrated was "made perfect"; it was "made new," was "dedicated." It was an act of separation from a common to a sacred use. Consecrated lives are always separated lives—separated from the common things of man to the sacred things of God. Such lives are "made new"; they are "going on unto perfection." This is the only pathway, the only route.

Consecration is based upon love. Without the latter there is no expression or exemplification of the former. Outward expressions of love are manifest on every hand. A short visit on a Sabbath afternoon to the English cemetery in Florence afforded manifestations of this affection. The grave of Theodore Parker is there, with a modest tombstone at its head, but with a symbolic torch on the topmost point of the stone. These words are chiseled thereon:

> "HIS NAME IS ENGRAVED IN MARBLE
> HIS VIRTUES IN THE
> HEARTS OF THOSE HE HELPED TO FREE
> FROM THE SLAVERY OF
> SUPERSTITION"

It seems strange that two such devoted lovers in wedlock as were Robert Browning and Elizabeth Barrett Browning, should, when death parted them, be laid to rest in such widely separated places as Westminster Abbey and this Florentine burying ground. Such was the case. Near by the central path, not very far from Parker's tomb, is the rather inconspicuous spot which marks the grave of that rare and gifted poetess, Mrs. Robert Browning. When we stood there, this was what, among other things, we viewed: There were two roses laid over her tomb, placed there by two admirers from Cleveland and Philadelphia. There was a card with this inscription, "Browning lovers, from Baylor University." Beneath, there were these words—words which have taught me the lesson of consecration—"How we love your clay." Well, yes, the Christian consecrates because he loves. He loves not "the clay" of

Christ, but the Cross and the claims of Christ. Before we can make a strong appeal for consecrations, we will have to deal with the problem of our love and our affections. "Do you love Me?" Man daily answers that question.

The consecration of self faces the mastership of our Lord. The problems of the former must deal with the process of the latter. The mastership of Jesus concerns the fellowship of Christians. If his mastership over us is perfected, our fellowship with him will not be neglected. Whatever else Jesus may have been to his disciples, by their frequent use of the word, he was surely their Master. Others than the disciples addressed him as "Master." The Greek word bears the meaning of Teacher, but he was more than a Teacher to his disciples. He was their Leader, their Guide, their Helper, their tender, kind-hearted, sympathetic Master. Martha the Domestic announced to Mary the Devoted, "The Master is here." In a desire to know how eternal life might be attained, the one whose business and profession it was to practice law addressed him as "Master." Startled by the announcement of betrayal plans from the lips of their Lord, the disciples came back with their accustomed speech, "Master, is it I?" Yonder on transfiguration's mount were the inner three of Jesus' cabinet. Delightful, romantic, hopeful moment it was! They would fain abide there, and the spokesman of the discipleship said: "Master, it is good for us to be here; . . . let's just live here all the time." Evidently Jesus loved and appreciated the name, for he said, after the Supper when the foot-washing scene occurred, "Ye call me Master—*and ye say well.*" One of the most personal appearances our Lord made to any of his followers was on the morning of Christianity's most signal victory. The women had come in search of their departed Master. In their perplexity he appeared to them (he always comes in perplexity's hour, if the faithful desire his presence!) and said, "Mary." In the glow of her discovery she used the same familiar word, "Master," and rushed toward him.

Not only is this word used often in theology, but the frequency of its use is witnessed in hymnology. Its use by the discipleship brought it into increasing prominence and popularity. Hymnists began to place it midst their tunes. This is happily being continued. "Master, the tempest is raging," wrote one hymnist. It was Washington Gladden, great Congregationalist, who penned:

> "O Master, let me walk with Thee
>   In lowly paths of service free;
>   Tell me Thy secret; help me bear
>   The strain of toil, the fret of care."

Dr. Frank Mason North, formerly Secretary of the Board of Foreign Missions of the Methodist Episcopal Church, feeling the great need of the gospel among the masses of our cities, penned his immortal words:

> "O Master, from the mountain side,
>   Make haste to heal these hearts of pain,
>   Among these restless throngs abide,
>   O tread the city's streets again."

Christian hymnody throughout the world has been brightened and gladdened by its interpretation of the mastership of our Lord.

This mastership of Jesus was not the ruler type. It was not the landlord type. Nor was it the overseer type. It was not a cold-blooded lordship, neither was it the proprietor type. The mastership of Jesus wooes and wins the discipleship of man. To Jesus, mastership meant a sympathetic Lordship, a vicarious Saviourship. It meant a costly Redeemership, resulting in a worthy ownership—the ownership of his own. Redemption was the cost of his earned mastership. His mastership to man means our sonship, our discipleship, and an intimate, constant type of fellowship.

My earliest recollection is the burning to the ground of the home of my nativity, when I had reached the advanced age of three years. This caused my father later to move to the county seat town. His farm was placed in the hands of a faithful colored man by the name of "Dee Bonner." This old hired man was doing his best with the farm; but my father did not think that the old Negro was meeting with any great amount of success in his agricultural endeavors, and informed Dee of his keen disappointment. The dear old man broke down and cried, weeping as humbly as an old slave, and said, with the hot tears streaming down his darkened face: "Boss, I'se sorry—and Boss, I'll go out in dat ar' orchid and git the biggest lim' you want me to git, and let you wear it out on me." A child's impression of God was to be gained! I was not over four and a half years of age when, sitting in the old family buggy, I heard that conversation between landlord and hired man. I think the tender eyes of my illustrious father grew moist when he said, "No, Dee; I'm not going to whip you; I just want you to take better care of things on the farm." "Yes, Boss; I'll do better." My father was his master, with a great, big, warm, human heart and a sympathetic understanding. This is what I mean when I speak of mastership. This is what I have in mind when I insist upon consecration. One was the master who deserved better service. The other was the servant who pledged to be more faithful. Is not that a picture of Christ? Is not that a picture of his disciples? Is not that a picture of God, a picture of you and of me? I think it must be!

Lord Kelvin, great English scientist, was once asked by a pompous young would-be scientist which one of all his discoveries he considered the most valuable. The unexpected reply was: "I think that to me the most valuable of all discoveries I have ever made was when I discovered my Saviour in Jesus Christ." With truth, I can say that one of the most valuable discoveries in my spiritual life which I have ever made has been the discovery of the compassion and tenderness of Jesus. I have seen them in the face of my father. I see this portrait to-day upon the countenance of God. Notice how often the Scriptures say, "He had compassion." A friend, walking with Lord Tennyson one day, said to the great poet laureate, "What is Christ to you?" The great poet and thinker paused and, placing his hand on a rose, said: "He is to me what the sun is to this flower. He is my life." So is he to me. This explains my devotion to the Communion Service.

The soul of Dr. F. B. Meyer has so recently gone home to God. But the spotless life and saintly influence of this immaculate soul live on. They will not down. One of the famous and soul-stirring stories which he told upon one of his Christian crusades in the States was the rather personal relation of the complete dedication of his life, and consecration of his service to Christ. He related that at a particular spiritual epoch in his career he determined faithfully and fearlessly to make an accurate accounting of his spiritual life. As he sat in quiet meditation, analyzing the disappointments and defeats of his highest spiritual purposes and endeavoring to discover the reason for his lack of spiritual power, Jesus Christ seemed to walk into the room and stand beside him. Evidently aware of the sincerity of this seeker for truth, Jesus asked Mr. Meyer to give him *the keys of his life*. This request from Christ was evidently with the intent that he should thereafter have complete and continuous access to every compartment and department of his life, so as to cleanse, control, and consecrate it to the purposes of God. Hesitating somewhat to accede to Christ's request, Mr. Meyer found in the face of Christ the hope and help he needed, and,

suiting the action to the word, he took from his pocket a
bunch of keys and handed them to Christ. Reaching forth
his hand, Christ took the keys, examined them carefully,
and then began to count them one by one. It was a searching but sacred time.

At last, so the account goes, Jesus looked upon his
friend, just as, centuries ago, he looked upon Peter when
something had gone wrong, and finally said to Mr. Meyer,
"Are they all here?" That was the critical question. That
was the question most difficult to answer conscientiously.
Could it be answered in the affirmative? The question
waited for the answer which was to test to the depths the
reality of this spiritual interrogation. There had been one
room in Mr. Meyer's life, so he said, in which he had har-
bored secret desires and fostered certain secret hopes.
He did not believe that Christ could approve of these desires and hopes, providing he was permitted to have absolute control of them. Somehow it was thought that if
Christ had all the other keys to all the other rooms, he
ought to be content. Nevertheless, Christ pressed the
question, "Are they all here?" Reluctantly, and with half
apology, the faint reply came, *"All but one."* It was such
a small one, but it was one. If Christ were shut out of
that room, if Christ could not have that one last key, he
could not be in control of that life. So he tenderly, but
firmly, said: "No, I cannot take them. If you cannot trust
me with them all, you cannot trust me at all." Then, with
an infinite pathos in his face as he looked upon the man
before him, the keys were handed back. There they were
—"all but one."

Then Christ started to leave the room, not because he
wanted to go, but because there was nothing else for him
to do. He will not force himself upon us. He comes only
when he is welcomed, not only as a Guest, but as a Master. Fearing that if Christ once left the room, he might

not return, Mr. Meyer said to him in broken speech: "O Master mine, I do not seem to have the strength to give you all the keys. But if you will come and take that last key from my half-unwilling hand and help me to be willing, I will give it to you with all the rest." Immediately Christ's face lighted with a joy that comes only from God, and, coming near, he took the half-reluctant hand within his own, and, with a tenderness and gentleness known only to him, the last key was gently taken from the clinging palm and placed on the ring with all the other keys. Then, taking that last key, he unlocked the last door of the heart, but at once he cleansed it and *kept the key*. "Ever since," said Mr. Meyer, "the hours of sweetest communion I have had with Christ have been in that very room, the key to which I had so reluctantly yielded to Christ."

Is not this the secret of Christ's mastery? Is it not the heart of the consecration urgency? The "key story" was related to a group of college students some years ago by one who was an artist in the presentation of spiritual truths to youth. In the assembly was a Chinese student, who, when the opportunity was afforded, arose and, in broken, imperfect English, said: "Many times I have given to Jesus many keys. But one key I never yet give to Jesus, and that is the master key. I now give to Jesus the master key to my life." Those words sent an electric thrill, with a spiritual exclamation, through the student audience, and they broke out in singing, "All hail the power of Jesus' name—and *crown him Lord of all*."

The Master is on a search for the key to each of the rooms of our lives. There is the dining room! Has Christ the key to that room? What is our spiritual food and fare? Do we try to feed our spiritual souls on the daily newspaper? If we do, it is poor spiritual diet. Does the monthly magazine, or the sporting page, or the page of "funnies," or the fashion journal, or the modern novel serve as our spiritual diet? Christ must have the key to the room of our appetites! The key to the art gallery, where our pictures are painted and hung up to view, has he the key to that room? Here the imagination works, and the portraits of the mind's handiwork are placed on the walls of the soul's art gallery. There is also the recreation, the social, room. Has Christ the key to that room? If so, the social problems of the life of the Church member and the Christian are solved. The Master insists that he must have the key to *every* room, or else he will not have the key to *any* room. He must be Master of all, if he is Master *at all*. It was Frances Havergal, in a midnight hour, after a signal spiritual victory, who penned a sermon in song in her

> "Take my life, and let it be
> Consecrated, Lord, to Thee."

There is no hymn in our knowledge which possesses more gospel, nor one which presents a keener and more effective appeal for the consecration of the entire life than Miss Havergal's hymn. A simple message presented by a humble lay woman who used the substance of this hymn for the material of her prayer meeting talk finally led me into the ministry. No wonder I love it!

In the section of the Church where my labors happen to fall, our bishop has been leading us in a series of "Spiritual Life Conferences." Only spiritual matters have been considered. No appeals for campaigns, for organizations, for money were in order. The spiritual needs were uppermost in our considerations. The Conferences, which usually were composed of two representative laymen and the minister from each charge in two or three districts, were divided into groups, which met at different times for personal conversation on the needs of their own souls. As the brethren gave their testimonies, and spoke of their problems of the spiritual life, more than a few gave this testimony: "I have a hard time keeping the quiet hour. I find myself reading the Bible for sermonic material rather than for soul help, unconsciously so." God came very close in some of those holy moments when hearts throbbed together. I am wondering to-day if we "men of the cloth" have given to Christ the key to our studies? I am asking if we have kept that first appointment of every morning with Him, as the Guest of that study? Other engagements of the day *must* be met. Shall this first engagement be omitted? How can we, as ministers, speak *for* Christ on Sunday unless he speaks *to* us on Monday and the other days of the week? The key to the study? The preacher's private, personal key! The key to his holy of holies! If the pulpit be our throne, the study must be our shrine. If the pulpit be the manifestation of power, the study must be the enduement of power. Rena Lloyd Humphreys, in an inspired poem on "The Study," said in one of the trenchant verses:

"Each morn I find in the dear little room new courage to live and be
  Faithful and true and give to the world the best that there is in me.
  Each night I kneel in the dear little room ere I close my eyes in rest;
  I feel a presence beside me there and know that my work is blest."

Transformations are made at Communion altars when consecrations are experienced at these sacred shrines. One of the early masterpieces which came from the hand of Michelangelo was a sermon in sculpture, his "David." As a youth, Angelo was stirred by the eloquence of Savonarola, and he never threw off the spell of that martyr soul. His magnificent "David" was begun two or three years after Savonarola's death, and may have been suggested by that militant prophet. For four hundred years his production stood near the spot where Savonarola was burned. Because of the exposure to the weather, it was in 1882 removed to the Academy of Fine Arts. It is related that Michelangelo saw a discarded stone upon which other sculptors had worked, and said, "I see an angel in that rock." He had it brought from its discarded environment, and placed his chisel to work upon the marble slab. His production is all the more remarkable because it was carved from one single block of marble about twenty feet high. But there his "David" stands—a muscular, overgrown lad, with the head of a youth and the feet and hands of a man. With the calm eye, the poised body, the steady hand upon his sling, he seems ready to meet his enemy, Goliath. One thinks of the words of Sir Galahad, "My strength is as the strength of ten, because my heart is pure," as he looks upon this masterpiece in marble. The "angel in the rock" was produced by a master of the chisel, because it was usable in the sculptor's hand. There are "angels" yet to be carved by the Master of the cross from the monolithic marble slabs of our lives if Christians are willing to be placed under his mastership. Jesus led us through the vale of consecration. Communion is the result.

"Give of your best to the Master;
    Give of the strength of your youth;
Throw your soul's fresh, glowing ardor
    Into the battle for truth.

Jesus has set the example;
    Dauntless was He, young and brave;
Give Him your loyal devotion,
    Give Him the best that you have."

IX

A STUDY IN ART

RUDYARD KIPLING, in his appealing poem "L'Envoi," speaks of the painting of "earth's last picture" by artists who

". . . shall find real saints to draw from—
    Magdalen, Peter, and Paul;
They shall work for an age at a sitting
    And never be tired at all."

And then this English poet, writer of famous lines, speaks of the Master praising his workmen for their efforts, and concludes by saying:

"And no one shall work for money,
    And no one shall work for fame;
But each for the joy of the working,
    And each, in his separate star,
Shall draw the Thing *as he sees It,*
    For the God of things as They are."

Artists have splashed "at a ten-league canvas with brushes of comet's hair" in an endeavor to portray their innermost impressions of the occurrences of the Last Supper. Sculptors of the world have given vent to their feelings, and have written in stone and on priceless slabs of marble their conception of the happenings of the night of that "Banquet of the soul." The poets have almost run wild, and the musicians have taken up the chorus with them, in their endeavor to portray in meditative lines and soulful notes that which they conceived to be the meaning of the last full attendance of the disciples with their Master at supper time. Carvers in wood, being led by the world-famous Lang family, have depicted their impressions by the slant of their sharpened knives and their keener consciences. The historians and the theologians have echoed back their interpretations of that eventful hour. All have joined in a heroic endeavor to "draw the Thing as he sees It." Some have pitifully failed. Others have met with glorious success, and those who have lived after them have been the glad recipients of their priceless benefactions.

Mankind is endowed with at least four insatiable cravings. He must have physical nourishment, and have it with a degree of regularity. He is possessed with a craving for knowledge. The more he knows, the more he desires to know. His craving for goodness is insatiable. Thus it has been said, with more or less truth, that "man is incurably religious." The better he is, the better he desires to be. He thus will "press on." And, then, mankind is endowed with an insatiable craving for the beautiful in life. When Beauty walks his way, he opens his eyes to behold her. He would clasp her hand in his in a desire to know art.

This Communion Meditation concerns the announcement of the betrayal. A later chapter will deal with the execution of the betrayal. Artists of many times and climes have endeavored to present to an art-loving and a Christ-devoted world their conceptions of this occasion in the life of our Lord and his Apostles. Bassano, whose painting of the Last Supper hangs in the Madrid Museum, pictures Judas with his back to the spectator, while in the angle of the supper table a dog and cat are quarreling over a bone. Other artists bring out the same idea of quarreling. There was discord there, but Jesus was never guilty of quarreling with his disciples. They quarreled with each other. It is interesting to note that Judas has his back to the spectator. Can we blame Judas for having such a desire as was depicted by Bassano? There was a lack of harmony there. Then I only ask—what better place is afforded the modern Christian to settle disputes with his Lord, with his neighbor, with his Church, than at Communion altars? Friction vanishes at that place of prayer! Devotees of Christ have arisen from such altars to go and make necessary restitution. They knelt in weakness. They arose with clean hearts, and purposes strengthened by the Spirit.

Bonifazio causes Christ to have his hand on the shoulder of St. John, while the "disciple whom Jesus loved" is reclining with his head upon the table. When one stands in the Uffizi Galleries in Florence and studies this painting, he walks away saying: "That is so much like Jesus' actions. That is so true of John."

Gebhardt, whose "Last Supper" is seen in the National Gallery, Berlin, represents Christ in the center of the table, with his left hand raised. At the right is John, who inquiringly places his hand upon the Saviour's arm. On the other side is James, the son of Alpheus, with his hand upon his mouth, looking searchingly at his Master. Nathanael, risen from his seat, is standing behind him. At the left, next to John, are sitting Simon Zelotes, Andrew, and James, the son of Zebedee. In the foreground, right, is Matthew trying to console the youthful Thomas, who hides his face in his hands, weeping. At the left is Judas, looking down sadly. Next to him is the empty chair of Judas Iscariot, who has risen and, noticed only by Bartholomew, is leaving the room. Wonder why the artist did not allow more of the disciples, possibly the whole group, with Christ included, to look upon the to-be-betrayer as he took his exit? Would the artist insist upon courtesy by the group? Would he portray that the leaving of the twelfth disciple was too saddening for many of them to witness his departure? Or, did Judas just slip out, and was Bartholomew the only one who chanced to see him?

Needless to say, there was action, and much of it, in that hour.

Andrea del Sarto's conception of the "Last Supper" is on display in a convent near Florence. His composition is rather similar to that of Da Vinci's masterpiece. Christ and the disciples are being seated on the same side of the table. Judas, at the right of Jesus, is protesting his innocence, while the rest show their astonishment and indignation. Tintoretto, whose work can be studied in Venice, causes the eleven disciples to be listening intently to Christ's words, while one of them, possibly Judas, is stopping to help himself to wine from a flask on the floor. This artist has another painting of the "Supper" in which he omits the presence of Judas entirely. In so doing he does an injustice to the record, for "he sat down with the *twelve*." Needless to say, there was a mixture of interest and diversity of purpose among the group. Eleven held on to Christ's words. One went away to carry them out, to put them into action.

If not the *most* famous, one of the most famous paintings of the "Last Supper" is the one which was executed by that gifted Italian, Leonardo da Vinci. Back of this painting lies a story, the story of a man and his contributions to the age in which he lived. All the intellectual curiosity of the Renaissance, its dreams of glory and of infinite progress, its enthusiasm for science and for beauty, were combined with many other attributes of genuis in Leonardo. Born in Vinci, between Pisa and Florence, in 1452, he was thus surrounded by many of the great souls of his day and age. The richest gifts are occasionally seen to be showered, as by celestial influence, on certain human beings; nay, they sometimes supernaturally and marvelously congregate in one sole person; beauty, grace, and talent being united in such a manner that to whatever the man thus favored may turn himself, his very action is so divine as to leave all other men far behind him. This was seen and acknowledged by all men in the case of Leonardo da Vinci, in whom there was a grace beyond expression which was rendered manifest without thought or effort in every act and deed, and who had besides so rare a gift of talent and ability, that to whatever subject he turned his attention, however difficult, he presently made himself absolute master of it. He not only worked in sculpture, but in architecture. He, at one time, recommended himself to the Duke of Milan as an inventor of engines of war, a builder of movable bridges, and as an engineer. He even believed that he had made a practical design for a flying machine. His musical abilities were especially manifested on the lute, excelling all others in this field of competition. He also recommended himself to the Duke as a painter, saying, "I can do as much as any other."

Leonardo's painting of the "Last Supper" was made for the Dominican monks of Santa Maria delle Grazie, at Milan. It was painted in oil on the walls of the refectory five years after a brother Italian from a neighboring city discovered America. This painter did nothing with simplicity, and the kind of oil used was a complicated cuisine predestined to scale and blacken. To the heads of the Apostles in this picture the master gave so much beauty and majesty that he was constrained to leave that of Christ unfinished, being convinced that he could not impart the divinity which should appertain to and distinguish an image of the Redeemer. The head of the Saviour he could not hope to find on earth, and he had not yet attained the power of presenting it to himself in imagination, with all that perfection of beauty and celestial grace which appeared to him to be demanded for the due representation of the Divinity incarnate.

It is further related that a second head, that of Judas,

was wanted by the artist, since he did not think it possible
to imagine a form of feature that should properly render
the countenance of a man who, after so many benefits received from his Master, had possessed a heart so depraved
as to be capable of betraying his Lord. The head of Judas
was finished successfully after he impersonated in art an
acquaintance who had treated him unjustly. This head,
indeed, became the image of treachery and wickedness.
Rather interesting to think that the artist was arrested in
his quest for two heads, one of impurity, the other of
purity; one of sinfulness, the other of sinlessness. I do
not wonder that he halted his brush in the endeavor to
portray either of the characters! It is said that the head
of Christ was finished by the hand of another. However,
authorities in art deny this statement, and are convinced
that he finished the Christ head as far as he did the other
heads; but he undoubtedly felt that it never was, and never
could be, completed to his own satisfaction. It is not to
be wondered that he came to this conclusion. It is hard
to paint purity. It is hard to picture divinity in oil colors.
Its best presentation is in the life of God in the soul of
man.

The admirable excellence of this painting is the beauty
of its composition and the care with which it was executed.
Leonardo succeeded to perfection in expressing the doubts
and anxiety evidenced by the Apostles, and the desire felt
by them to know by whom their Master is to be betrayed.
In the faces of all appear love, terror, anger, or grief and
bewilderment, unable as they are to fathom the meaning of
their Lord. Nor is the spectator less struck with admira-
tion by the force and truth with which, on the other hand,
the master has exhibited the impious determination, hatred,
and treachery of Judas. The whole work is executed with
inexpressible diligence even in its most minute part.
Among other things may be mentioned the tablecloth, the

texture of which is copied with such exactitude that the linen cloth itself could scarcely look more real.

It will be seen upon further study that the disciples are arranged in groups of three, on each side of Christ, who occupies the middle place at the table. On His right is the first group, John, Judas, and Peter. Jesus has just announced that "one of you shall betray me." The artist has caught the psychological moment. Look at Jesus! With the announcement, his hands are outstretched, lying on the table, while his eyes—the eyes which looked upon Jerusalem—the eyes which looked upon every one of the twelve three years previously when he called them into the ministry—his eyes are cast gently down. He is too courteous to look at the betrayer. What a courtly man was Jesus! He is most too sorrowful to face his family in the eye. He looks as though he would ask himself, "God, is it possible that one of *my own* is to betray me?" "The beloved," with eyes closed beneath a youthful brow, has his head slightly reclining. Judas is drawing back, leaning upon the table, with the bag tightly clenched in his fist. While Peter, with characteristic action, leans forward with his hand on John's shoulder, with the other hand holding a knife. They all are asking, "Lord, is it I?"

The second group to the Master's right is composed of Andrew, James the younger, and Bartholomew, who is standing. Andrew's hands are upraised slightly, portraying wonder and amazement. James, with his arm on Andrew's shoulder, the other hand raised in horror, looking much like the Christ, seems to be saying for his group, "Master, is anyone in this group going to betray you?" To the left of Christ are grouped James the elder, Thomas, and Philip. James, with opened arms and dazed expression, Thomas, with inquiring, upraised finger, and Philip, with arms clasped across his breast and with head bent toward the Saviour, all unite in the interrogation as to whom it was who would hang dishonor upon himself in the act of betrayal. The last group, consisting of Matthew, Thaddeus, and Simon, seem to be talking to themselves rather than to Christ. They seem to be arguing, questioning, almost wrangling. It is the marvelous expression upon the face of each member of the group that gives the painting its excellence. The food lies on the table unnoticed and seemingly undesired. The impression of increasing excitement and commotion grows as one gazes upon the masterpiece of Da Vinci. The only one who seems to be undisturbed is Jesus. He appears to be calm and masterful, yet he seems sorrowful. When one stands in the presence of this painting and observes and studies its intimate details, he invariably asks himself, "Master, is it *I?*" It is not only a great work of art, but a page of the profoundest psychology, a study of character and feeling, translated at once by the expressions of the faces, the gestures, and the attitudes. More concerned am I to-day about the expressions of modern communicants, their gestures, and their attitudes in the presence of, and toward, this Sacrament of the Soul.

It is more interesting to see this great artist as he approaches the unknown crossing of life. His last three years were spent in France in the service of the King of France. Having become old, he lay sick for many months, and, finding himself near death, he wrought diligently to make himself acquainted with the Catholic ritual and with the path of religion, so records Giorgio Vasari. He then confessed with great penitence and many tears, and, although he could not support himself on his feet, yet, being sustained in the arms of his servants and friends, he devoutly received the Holy Communion while out of bed. Thus did he who had presented a masterpiece in art on the Sacrament to a Christ-seeking world wait till he was near death's door to partake of its spirit. He had barred himself from this Sacrament. Barred by his own hands! He had exposed himself to its *exterior* form rather than to its *interior* force. Pity the modern Christian who only partakes of the exterior of Communion without its soulful interior grace and influence! The real artistry of the Sacrament cannot be painted with brush and oils. One must go deeper than that; yea, to the inner altars of the mystic heart of man.

Penitence found its way in the life of Da Vinci ere he put away his brush to splash no more. The King of France heard of his illness, and, as he was accustomed to do, visited the great artist. His visits were characterized by frequency and affection. When the King entered, Leonardo, causing himself, out of reverence, to be raised up, sat in bed describing his malady, lamenting, besides, that he had offended God and man, inasmuch as he had not labored in art as he ought to have done. The spirit of the artist departed to meet that of the other Artist, we trust, as Leonardo rested in the arms of the King. May it be that from the arms of one king his spirit went to the arms of another King—him who was called "King of the Jews!" "The Painter Dying at Fontainebleau in the Arms of Francis I" is the name of the original painting, which hangs to-day in the Louvre, depicting the artist's death.

More interesting than this, perhaps, is the present state of this world's masterpiece. The colors faded rapidly. It was repainted in 1726 by Bellotti. It was again repainted in 1770 by Mazza; and in 1853 was retouched by Barozzi. The lower part of the central group was destroyed in 1652 when a door was cut through the wall. And in 1793 the refectory was made into a stable. Napoleon's cavalrymen stabled their horses in this building, seemingly all unconscious of the rich treasure on the wall besmattered with filth. It is said that the little Corsican objected to this being done. When one reads Ludwig's "Life of Napoleon," he is almost inclined to doubt if this military genius cared a trifle whether or not the refectory was turned into a stable or else completely destroyed. We will accept the verdict of the historian, and give the great warrior all the credit which he is due. His respect for the Church of Christ was decidedly below par, at that.

Not only was the painting damaged by dragoons, but in 1800 the refectory was flooded for fifteen days. It is a wonder that the painting as it is revealed to-day is in such a state of preservation, despite the talented retouches of the hands of devoted and gifted artists. A good work in *Christian* art, the art of the soul, can be done, and needs to be done, by the devotees of Christ in this day. It needs to be retouched, to be repainted with the renewed oils, colors, and paints of our undying loyalty and fealty. It has been marred by the dragoons of the critics. It has been scarred by the unholy attacks upon its spiritual efficacy and power. It has been barred by the tangled wires of indifference. It has been battered, tattered, and scattered. How it has been flooded by the tidal waves of unconcern, and for many days—and many years—has been so deeply immersed that too little thought has been given to its beneficent presentation to modern communicants. Yet it has borne the battle scars and to-day stands out as the freshest Sacrament of the Christian Church despite its antiquity.

I am happy to join that caravan, that multitude of cherished souls, who dare to stake the chances of their eventual and eternal salvation upon its efficacy. Despite the fact that this Sacrament has been so criticized, I will rest the hope of my peace upon its soothing, life-giving poise and uplifting power. It becomes the high and holy duty, and the sacred privilege, of "priest and people" of modern Christendom to give to the painting the retouches which it needs. Christians, ministers, followers of a sacrificing Lord, get your brushes and paint it anew in 1932! If there be faded spots in the Painting—and there are—we must retouch them with the red blood of life's courage, with the whitened purity of our life's devotion. With such colors as these it cannot fade. These are indelible. Imperishable are these!

In such a degraded, repainted, and fading condition as has been described Leonardo da Vinci's masterpiece now stands. To-day the orginal is but a shadow of a shade of the original perfection of which we can best judge by the fine drawing for the head of Christ, in the Brera, and to some extent by the copy of Marco d'Oggione, in the Royal Academy, London. May it be forbidden that the original Supper becomes a *shadow* or a *shade!* The artist endeavored through many months, through years, to make a copy of the original Supper. Immediately over my study desk, as I write, hangs a copy of Leonardo's original. It cheers me. It awes me. It thrills me. It soothes me. It causes me to kneel in humiliation. It makes me sing with hope and pray with trust. It causes me to arise and ask, "Lord, is it I?" After all, the best copy of Christ's original teaching of loyalty, devotion, fealty, and sacrifice cannot be splashed upon a waiting canvas by the gifted hand of the talented; but the real original may be splashed across the canvas of life's heroic activities in the living of a life in conformity with the teachings and ideals of Him who said, "One of you shall betray me." That is the copy which becomes the holy task for the Church of this day to produce. It will not fade. It endures. Charles Wesley, Methodism's most gifted singer, gave us the ideal in theology and poetry; Louis Spohr placed the lines to music:

"A heart in every thought renewed,
    And full of love divine;
Perfect, and right, and pure, and good,
    A copy, Lord, of Thine!"

X

EARTH'S BLACKEST NIGHT

Does "THE SHADOW OF THE CROSS lie athwart the manger crib"? The previous Meditation dealt with the foregleams of the betrayal. The burden of this chapter has to do with the light—or, shall I say, the midnight blackness?—of the betrayal, and the execution of betrayal intentions. Previously, we faced a Supper. Now, we face a Cross. Previously, we faced a Family. Now, we face a mob. Before, there was a stillness, accompanied with a shock. Now, there is a bang, a blast, and a quiver. The "shadow of the Cross" lay athwart that Supper scene. There is an intimate acquaintance — yea, a personal kindredship — between the Supper and the Cross. There would have been no Supper had it not been followed by a Cross. Had there been no Cross in the background, there would have been no Supper in the foreground. Had there been no Christ on the Cross, there would have been no Christ at the Table.

The two scenes are inseparable. There must be both a Supper and a Cross for either to be efficacious. Either is lost without the other. The two experiences took place in the same city, separated by only a few hours and only a few city blocks. Pilate's Hall, with the marks of the gamblers in the floor to-day, is hard by the scene of the Passover night, and the "hill outside the city walls" lies only a distance of a few moments' walk. At the Supper the wine of remembrance was poured. On "a hill far away" the blood of his life was spilt. Upon that Passover night the bread of renewed strength was broken. On Golgotha his body was crushed, bruised, and broken for a world's redemption. No Cross? Then, no Supper! No

Sacrament? Then, no crucifixion! The Church errs, and leaves the track which Christ trod, if she refuses to make a close connection and preach a close relationship between these two epochal, soul-stirring experiences in the life of her Lord and Saviour. He who prayed at the Passover Table was soon to prostrate his soul at Gethsemane's altars, and later to bare his breast before an angry, ferocious mob on Calvary.

Was there ever such a night of activity? Was there ever so much commotion and stirring? The commotion began around the Supper table. It was to spread from that inner shrine with friends to the outer stir midst foes. "The Supper being ended," the devil placed it into the heart of Judas to betray Him. There was no place made for the evil one at the Table, but he pushed and urged his way into a small nook, and worked havoc. The physical doom of Jesus was thus sealed *at the Table*. It is then possible for evil desires to be entertained as we kneel at modern Communion altars! Jesus knew "who should betray him," and with the knowledge he began to wash the disciples' feet. A text which has too long been omitted in our dissertations are those symbolic words of the soon-to-be-Crucified, "He took a towel." One of the great bishops of Methodism, now gone to his deserved reward, had a compelling sermon on that significant text.

With the execution of the Master's desire to wash his disciples' feet, came these words, "He that eateth bread with me hath lifted up his heel against me." And the Record says, "Jesus was troubled." How could he be otherwise and retain his humanity? "That thou doest, do quickly," were his words. "He then, having received the sop, went immediately out." What a masterly handling of the situation it was. This is a picture of the artistry of His mastery. He literally helped the betrayal along and relieved Judas of the necessity of the announcement of his intentions. There seems to be a pause in the account. John's record says, *"and it was night."* If the betrayal was to be, *night* was the best time. Daylight was too bright. Too much could be seen. Darkness was the most appropriate time—if there could be an appropriate time for such a deed. I think the Syrian moon must have put her hands over her face and draped herself in mourning. I have always imagined that the wind must have howled its mournful dirge—for there was a funeral in the offing. Requiem it must have been! "It was night." Blackness abounded. A black deed—the blackest in the world's history—was just over the sunrise of the approaching day of horrors and sorrows, the day of hilarity and calamity.

In the darkness of that night Judas had a sale. He gambled away his God. He sold his soul. He forfeited his fortune. It used to be that the blackest deeds were done in the blackness of the night. Not so in this day of sunrise hold-ups and noonday crimes. With Judas the night was the time of the execution of his satanic plans. Was there ever such a pathetic creature as Judas? Dean Charles R. Brown calls him "the man who might have been." He was one who grew worse in personal character while others, under the identical influences, grew better. Judas was a gamble to his Lord. But, it has been also suggested that, as for that matter, all the group of disciples was a gamble to Christ. Judas is a vivid picture of an ugly process of a moral decline. The "set of his sails" was wrong. They were too mercenary. He became "the apostle with the broken neck." He helped to slay his Lord.

The soul of Judas, his reputation, and his waning life were bought for a contemptible collection of "thirty pieces of silver." For that sum he auctioned off his crown. It is said that when the liquor men of the United States were looking for a lawyer to represent their interests and to combat constitutional prohibition in the courts, they approached Hon. Charles E. Hughes, offering him a retaining fee of $150,000. Showing much resentment that they would even think of him as available for such service, he indignantly replied, "I would not champion this cause before the courts for any sum of money you could name." Then they sought an interview with Hon. William Howard Taft. Instead of offering him a stated amount of money, they handed him a blank check, telling him to fill in any amount he wished. Mr. Taft had an opportunity that moment of becoming a millionaire, but it was not to him the slightest temptation. He promptly said to them: "Gentlemen, you couldn't pile enough gold on this continent to induce me to take your case before the courts, and before the public, for I will have you to know *my conscience is not for sale.*" And what places of trust and admiration and worth these two gentlemen have held in this nation!

It is also related that, at the close of the bitter War between the States, the Louisiana Lottery Company offered Gen. Robert E. Lee the sum of ten thousand dollars a year —a very large sum in those days—if he would consent to become the president of that organization. This great Christian statesman and soldier replied: "Gentlemen, all I have in this world at the close of this cruel war is my good name and my principles, and they are not for sale. I cannot accept your offer." But Judas accepted. He received a cash payment. He paid the penalty.

A prayer meeting was held that night. Three were "to watch" with Him, but their lack of appreciation of the meaning of that hour, and the upheaval of physical weariness, caused them to fall on slumber. Beneath the sympathetic hoverings of Gethsemane's olive trees the battle of Christ's soul was fought. The "not my will, but thine, be done" was said only after everything of humanity, and everything of Divinity, which he possessed, came into play.

On the western slope of the Mount of Olives rests this battle ground. Its trees are scarred and gnarled, aged, torn and worn. The hot blasts of Palestine's breezes, mixed with an occasional snowfall, have beaten upon their olive branches. But still they live and grow. They tell of God, and of God's Son who prayed one night—not for the world, but for himself alone. These trees are bent, and deformed, weighted with age, to such an extent that it is almost impossible for them to support their own weight. They are unquestionably many hundreds of years old, and may have possibly been standing at the time of Christ. A few green branches are the only indication that they still contain life; but under the devoted care of monks who have charge of the garden, they will no doubt live for many years to come. A visit to the Garden just before sunset rewards any visitor with an impressively quiet half hour. As a rule, a gorgeous sunset may be expected, framed in the overhanging branches of the ancient trees, with a silhouette of the walls and buildings of the Holy City sharply outlined against the paling sky. The everlasting attraction of the Garden is not its trees, nor its flowers, but the fact that God in flesh intimately pleaded with his Father before next morn's sun arose to announce the day of his crucifixion. Hofmann has immortalized this scene with his masterpiece, "Christ in Gethsemane."

In a certain Western city a strange thing happened one New Year's Eve, not many years ago. Suspended in the sky was a great cross of shimmering silver. There it was, a block long and quite wide, shining out in the blackness of the sky. Folks asked: "Is it a sign? What does it mean?" The mystery was soon figured away, for a cloud of frost was hanging over the town, and had caught the reflection of the lights of the two long streets of the little city. That explained the mystery, but it was uncanny and unbelievably beautiful. The explanation of the mystery did not rob the vision of its meaning. A cross over a city. Ah! there was a Cross over a Supper table. There was a Cross over a Garden which shone forth in the blackness of the Palestinian night. The vision of Christ outdistanced that of the disciples asleep without. When wine is poured and bread is broken and passed to devout communicants, there is the shadow of the cross overhanging those elements—and there always shall be!

The last steps in the execution of betrayal plans were brazen, yet there was an element of pathos and pity running through. "Hail, Master," cried the disciple, the betrayer, and kissed the Betrayed. A caress in Eastern lands corresponds with the handclasp in Western lands. It was an act of friendship, cordiality, and affection. Did the kiss of Judas on that black night possess any of these qualifications? That action was hypocrisy in its most brazen form. In contrast with this came the gentle word of the Betrayed, "Friend." Traitorship never seems so black and treacherous until it is placed on the whitened canvas of friendship. A lie never seems so debasing until it is placed beside the truth. Sinfulness never seems so ghastly until it is placed against sinlessness. Judas never seems so pitiful, so unholy, until he is placed next to Jesus, personification of purity, exemplification of holiness.

Judas was in the wrong kind of environment for intimate friendship with Christ. He "stood with them." With *whom* did he stand? Not with the disciples, his former colaborers and companions, whose money he had carried, and by whom he had labored and slept. He was out of his accustomed pew. He was with the soldiers and the crucifiers, who had blood in their eyes and sin in their hearts. In his betrayal there was the aroma of Gethsemane's submission. In the betrayal there was the sound of Pilate's gavel calling the court to order for the trial of the morrow.

In the betrayal were the echoes of the voices near to-morrow's noon, crying: "Crucify him! Crucify him!" In the betrayal was the kindredship of Peter's "I know him not." In the betrayal was the reaction of the escape of Barabbas. In the betrayal was the hush of the calm which decked his manly brow as he stood his trial. In the betrayal was the halting which caused an exchange in cross-bearers on the morrow. In his betrayal were the sound of driven nails, the color of spurting blood, and the chug of a cross as it struck the bottom of its resting place. In the betrayal was the pressure of sweat "as drops of blood" on a faultless, aching brow, the story of which, from the lips of a godly mother, brought tears to the eyes of my early childhood. In the betrayal was the wonder of to-morrow's words, "Father, *why* hast Thou forsaken me?" In the betrayal was the echo of the words, "Forgive them . . . they know not what they do." In this blackened deed on a blackened night there ascended the aroma of vicarious words, "It is finished," as he dropped his head on a pulse-less breast, only to awaken "in the morning."

Goethe once exclaimed, "If I were God, sin would break my heart." That is what transpired in the life of Jesus. True it was that he died of physical pains and persecutions on the Cross, but never did man die with such heart throbs and heart-breakings as this "Man of Sorrows." His ac-quaintance had been personally, intimately, minutely made with pain. "Never man" experienced pain as did he, the One who relieved so many needy ones of their pains of body, mind, and soul. A Physician on a painless ministry! The pains He experienced *prior* to the Cross were com-parable to those experienced while on its rugged surface.

Christendom has called the day of his crucifixion "Good Friday." The ancient Scandinavians, Anglo-Saxons, and Germans regarded the day as a "lucky day." The Moham-

medans observe Friday as their day of worship. The
Roman, the Greek, and the Anglican Churches recognize
it as a day of abstinence, in memory of the crucifixion of
Christ. In more recent years Friday has been regarded
as an "unlucky day," as "hangman's day." To-day Good
Friday is called Great Friday in the Greek Church. Hence
this day, the Friday prior to Easter, is observed quite gen-
erally throughout the Christian world as a day of solemn
thought and deep meditation. Churches in increasing number are adopting the custom of conducting services from
noon until three o'clock, when the "Words of Christ from
the Cross" are spoken in sermon and sung in music. A
most appropriate time is afforded at the closing moments
of such a service for the commemoration of the Lord's
Supper.

Jesus was born with the print of the Cross on his heart,
and died with the imprint of the same on his back. He
was born in a rented stable, lived homeless, died on crucify-
ing crossbeams, and was buried in a borrowed tomb. It is
much easier to *wear* a cross than to *bear* a cross. The
Cross is not meant for decoration—it stands for consecration. Some one has truthfully said that "the Church could
save the world if she was not frightened by her crosses."
We have sung, rather lustily, in the yesteryears, "when the
battle's over, we shall wear a crown." But have we stopped
to think that the *wearing* of the crown is preceded by the
bearing of a cross? I stood, with uncovered head and
throbbing breast, in Bunhill Fields, that Silent City of the
Immortals, in London, containing, perhaps, more of the
dust of the noble dead than any other burial ground—
Westminster, London, excepted—to be found anywhere.
A reverent pause was made beside the last resting place of
Isaac Watts, immortal singer, crystal soul, producer of
theology and song, and from beneath the exterior these
words floated out:

"When I survey the wondrous cross
On which the Prince of glory died,
My richest gain I count but loss,
And pour contempt on all my pride."

Then I knew that Watts had the meaning of following
Christ in consecrated discipleship till death. Jesus said,
"If any man will come after me, let him deny himself,
take up his cross, and follow me." The Church of to-day
draws back from that verse. It would fain not deny herself. It would prefer not to take up her cross. Not so
with the early Christians. They carried their personal
cross. They courted the headman's axe. The cross to
them was their crown. To-day there is too much backing
off from our cross. This explains many of our spiritual
losses. The only way we can get into the inner shrine of
the Sacrament is through the portals of the cross. Some
Christians would accept the Sacrament more quickly than
the cross of the Sacrament. But there can be no genuine
acceptance of the Sacrament without a truthful acceptance
of the Cross.

Much of our use of the Cross has caused an abuse of
the Cross. Too long has the Cross been left out of our
living. Too long has the element of suffering been left
out of the Cross. It has been decorated and garnished till
in spots it is tarnished. We have illuminated the Cross,
but failed to apprehend it. One pastor used it so often in
Church services, decorating it in various ways, that some
of the most faithful attendants said, "There's that old
cross again." A superintendent of the Cradle Roll Department of a Sunday school, in an endeavor to secure
some usable coat racks for the children's hats, caps, and
coats, had three small coat racks made—in the form of a
cross—with screws in appropriate places. Crosses as coat
racks! A Methodist pastor says in his bulletin, in com-
menting upon a certain youth service: "The presence of the

great, ghastly cross with its dreadful nails cast a spell over the audience that could not be shaken off. Too long have we *beautified* the cross and *decorated* it until the fact of suffering has been almost effaced from it." Let us take the trimmings off, and preach and live the cross as it really was and is, and approach the Sacramental table through the doors of the Cross of the Crucified!

The Cross of Christ stands watch over a world in darkness—a beacon to bewildered souls. Of the famous Junaluska Cross, at Lake Junaluska, North Carolina, it has been written: "Blazed the Cross in the darkness of the night, no longer to me a thing of blood and superstition, but the great love emblem of the world—the divine unanswered challenge of the ages." It need not be a superstition, but every true cross has drops of blood on its surface. Every Easter morn is preceded by a night of darkness and a day of blood. There is no Easter without a Cross. Neither can we appreciate the Christian significance of the Easter lily, unless we sense the meaning of Good Friday's Cross and Saturday's tomb. Too many of us desire an Easter without a Thursday night, a Friday, and a Saturday. The glory of Easter dawn is always preceded by the gloom of these three days.

Rev. George Bennard has thrilled the Christian world with his "Old Rugged Cross." As I heard him sing it I felt his inner soul, and the pulse of the song. Jesus died "on a hill far away." So did Napoleon. Both were warriors, with opposite goals in view. Of Napoleon it has been said, "His only interests were in himself." Of Jesus it has been said, "He died for others." If ever man forgot himself, God's Son did.

> "Let self be crucified and slain,
> And buried deep may efforts be
> To rise again, unless
> To live for others."

On an extinct volcano in the Atlantic Ocean, two thousand miles from Europe and nearly a thousand miles from Africa, guarded by British guns, such is the rock of St. Helena upon which an outcast soldier lived for six years in exile. On this island no one lives to reach the age of sixty, and a very few reach the age of fifty. They who stay for a year suffer from dysentery, giddiness and fever, vomiting and palpitation. Whenever England tried to station a squadron on Helena for the purpose of guarding Napoleon, the sailors died by the hundreds. The exiled man lived in a home made out of a cowshed. His bedroom was furnished with a threadbare carpet, muslin curtains, a fireplace, painted wooden chairs, two small tables, a washstand, and a sofa. In exile he said: "Cæsar was assassinated. Hannibal committed suicide. I am banished from my homeland and will die in exile. Jesus Christ, a Jew, was crucified and died for the salvation of the world."

One of his biographers thus describes Napoleon's death: "With amazing energy he springs out of bed, overpowering Montholon—the two fall on the floor. He is unloosed from Napoleon's embrace by assistance of another. No one knows what enemy the Emperor was trying to strangle in this last fight. Mist and rain drive fiercely around the house. At five o'clock the rage of the southeast wind is redoubled, and two trees of the latest planting are uprooted. At this moment the man on the bed is in the throes of a prolonged rigor. There is no sign of pain. They moisten his lips with a sponge dipped in vinegar. His eyes are wide open, staring into vacancy. The death rattle is in his throat. As the tropical sun sinks into the sea, the Emperor's heart stops beating."

His last understandable words were the expressions of his pent-up emotions. He was thinking of those who had been dearest and nearest to him; those who had helped him when he needed assistance. His lips moved, and the word was "France, France." That was his beloved country, wherein his hand had manifested its most powerful sway and dominion. He longed to die in "France, France." Again the lips were seen to move. Listen what came forth! "Armee! Armee!" His "armee" had been the secret of his strength, as he had captured the affections and devotions of men. His army was his power, and, in death's agony, he desired that power. Once more, and this for the last time, his lips, which had commanded millions, moved to speak. This time it was of a personal love, a private affection. The woman whom he had divorced—but whom he loved—came before his eyes, and in the distinctness of the vision he said, almost without breath, "Josephine, Josephine." She was his lover. He was her lover. He would love her in death's grasp and in life's last hour.

I know Another, exiled He was from the help of Friendship's gladdening grasp. In the thirst of His lonely hour He cried out, and the mob stuck to His lips a sponge dipped in vinegar. The rage of the winds was blowing across that skull-shaped brow, and at His expiration the vale was rent in twain. The Record informs us that He spoke seven times from the cross. A portion of those sayings concerned His own personal self, his aching body and His weary heart. But more than all He was thinking of his country, his army, and his bride, "the bride of Christ," Christian soldiers who were to take up the battle where He left it off, and march on in the strength and urgency of His Good Name. "Alexander, Cæsar, Charlemagne, and I have founded great empires. But upon what did these creations of our genius depend? Upon force! Jesus alone founded his empire on love, and to this very day millions would die for him." And Napoleon was right!

XI

BEYOND THE TOMB

"Alone with Thee, amid the mystic shadows,
  The solemn hush of Nature newly born;
Alone with Thee in breathless adoration,
  In the calm dew and freshness of the morn.

Still, still with Thee! As to each newborn morning
  A fresh and solemn splendor still is given,
So does this blessed consciousness, awaking,
  Breathe each day nearness unto Thee and heaven."

MORN BREAKS! The glimmering tints of sunrise, slashed
with color, abundant in the eastern sky, announce the birth
of Another Day. Night has gone into retirement. Its
shadows have faded. Sorrow has been suddenly, but surely,
transformed into sunrise. Faith has met its glad fruition.
"The dew is still on the roses." Prophets' dreams have
come into the realm of realization. Jesus Christ, the Son
of God, is risen, for on Calvary his sun is set "to rise
again." Glorious hope is clutched victoriously to the breast
of believing, expectant souls! Easter morning brings us
beyond the tomb, this glad day which has been called "a
Sunday that walks like a jeweled queen in the midst of her
sister Sundays."

Redemption's morning was born on this hill called Calvary. Easter is the name which Christianity has given to
this day. The soul of the most unresponsive is usually
touched, and the hearts of the most devoted are inwardly
thrilled on Resurrection's Day. This day was preceded
by a Thursday night, by a Friday morning, afternoon, and
night, and by a Saturday of hopeful, watchful waiting.
The true interpretation of its sunrise cannot be appreciated

apart from the meaning of the sorrow, sacrifice, and silence
of the three previous days. One cannot appreciate the hope
of Easter without the horror of these three days. The
song of Easter comes to its rightful meaning as it is interpreted through the sorrow of Gethsemane. There would be
no Easter chorus unless it had been preceded by a funeral
dirge. The lily of Easter morning received its painting in
the love of the Supper night and the sacrifice of Good
Friday.

To-day—this glorious day—we are *beyond the tomb*.
We are beyond the betrayals, the denials, the agony, the
cross, the spittles, and the mockings. Beyond the tortures
and the trials, the crying and the dying. Beyond the woes
and the throes, the pains and the blames. Beyond the doom
and the gloom! Our mourning has been transformed into
a morning. Day-before-yesterday we looked upon an
occupied cross; to-day we behold an unoccupied tomb. On
the day-before-yesterday we looked into the agonizing face
of a suffering Christ; to-day we behold the peaceful countenance of a risen Redeemer. Previously there were the
bleeding heart and the pierced side; now there are the
glowing heart and the nail-printed hands. Before this day
there were the wail and the gore; but to-day there are the
"hail" and the glory. Previously there had been the gloom
and the shades of death; to-day there are the glow and the
certainty of a deathless morning. A silent pause on Resurrection's morning for the purpose of ascertaining the price
of this day of glory is decidedly worth while.

The deepest emotions and the fondest hopes of man lie
beyond the tomb. Upon this day Hope is realized; Hope
is grasped, and held within our personal possession. Hope
doth "spring eternal in the human breast." Recently there
came before my view an illustration in cartooned form.
The giant iceberg of atheism was afloat upon the bosom of
a darkened sea. Standing on its chilling surface was the

small form of a man. In the distance, with a light shining about it, was a sailboat, with "Faith in God" marked upon its sails. Above the picture was the inscription, "The World Needs Hope." Beneath were the words, "Having no hope, and without God in the world." This cartoon shows the most dismal of all human beings in eternity, with cold atheism for a companion. But on Resurrection's morn Hope comes into its own.

Upon the walls of Tate's Gallery, London, hangs G. F. Watts' interpretation of "Hope." Those who gaze upon this painting note that the exquisite curve of the bent figure seemingly suggests despair. "The blindfolded eyes are eloquent of a grief so sharp that it has died of its own sting, and only blank indifference is left." The broken and battered lyre speaks of a life whose music has been silenced—a dumb, savorless existence from which the very brutes might well draw back. Why, then, has Watts called such a picture Hope? Was it not that the artist buried his conception of hope somewhere behind the despairing curves, the blinded eyes, the drooping head, and the un-smiling face of the figure that sits so desolately upon the surface of a cold, irresponsive globe? Or, did the artist intend that the one unbroken string that is left on her lyre should symbolize the hope that survives the wreckage of all else? Hope is there "splashed" somewhere across the painting regardless of the interpretations of art lovers— it is there. In the sound of the one remaining, unbroken string it seems that the artist has placed his hope.

It was Paganini who, facing a crowded house of music lovers, broke every string on his violin except one, and with the confidence of a master violinist walked to the front of the rostrum and said, "Ladies and gentlemen, Paganini and one string," and music of rare beauty and gifted charm was produced by that one-stringed violin and the artist who held the bow and the instrument. John Fiske quotes

Job's saying, "Though he slay me, yet will I trust him," as the sublime and triumphant expression of faith. Resurrection is the proof of that faith. It is Hope realized. Over the triple doorways of the Cathedral of Milan there are three inscriptions spanning the magnificent arches. Over one are the words, "All that pleases is but for a moment." Over the other, "All that troubles is but for a moment." While over the central arch are these significant words—especially so, on Easter morning—"That only is important *which is eternal*." "And now abideth hope," said the great Apostle. It still abides, for it is eternal. Its eternity reached its justification at the tomb.

Not only does Hope lie beyond the tomb, but Life lies over there. Life experienced, not existence endured, lies beyond the tomb. The world had not yet seen life, life in all its elements of expression, until Resurrection's morning. If you would see Life, look at Jesus *beyond the tomb*. Jesus taught the world the meaning of immortality. He was Immortality itself. Some doubts arise concerning the details of the story, and so many have hidden behind Thomas who said, "I will not believe, except I shall see in his hands the print of the nails, and put my finger into the print of the nails, and thrust my hand into his side." And this sincere disciple of our Lord has been called "doubting Thomas." Perhaps I would have said similar words, or had the same attitude. The words of Thomas represented his *quest for reality*. Is such a quest to be denied to an honest disciple? We have remembered Thomas for his doubts rather than for his faith. Look a little closer. This follower of the Nazarene was not present with the disciples on the first appearance of their resurrected Lord in their midst. The second time he was there, and when the Master entered the room, it was Thomas whom he addressed. Jesus looked at his seeking disciple, and requested him to place his finger into the nail prints, and his hand into the gash made by the spear. John does not tell us that Thomas went through this procedure, but he does tell us of his declaration of his personal faith, when saying, "My Lord, and my God." The devils can say, "O God," but they cannot say "My God." This is a privilege peculiar to God's chosen people. As Thomas was looking for a nail-printed Christ, the world out yonder, outside of our Christian Churches, is looking for Christians with the print of the nails of Christian devotion and fearless fealty in their palms.

The Church has had much to say relative to the nature of the resurrection—whether it was a spiritual or a bodily resurrection. Millions of people constantly repeat, "I believe in the resurrection of the body, and the life everlasting." Battles have raged over the head of this creedal statement. They may continue to rage. The body of Jesus was entombed, carefully guarded, and three things might have taken place. (1) The body may have continued to lie in the grave. If so, did it stay there, and return to dust? Why, then, did not the foes of Jesus present it? Had this been the case, his disciples never would have gathered together again for their evangelistic, hopeful activities. (2) Was the body stolen away? It was Passover time, and a full moon was in the Syrian sky. Either friend or foe, who might have endeavored to steal it, would have been detected. If the enemies of Christianity had the body, why did they not produce it? If the disciples had it in their possession, how could they have gotten by the Roman guards? They did not possess enough physical strength to overpower the guards, nor enough money to bribe them. Had the disciples secured the body by bribery or by force, why were they not indicted for their theft? If the disciples possessed the body, from whence came their new found faith and their new courage to establish Churches in many places? (3) The body did rise from

the dead. For the grave was empty. The disciples saw
the empty grave; Paul did not. The testimony of the
former must have taken precedence over that of the latter.
The body of Jesus was seen by more than five hundred
people after the resurrection. A Moslem said to Stanley
Jones: "We go to Arabia and find the tomb of our Prophet,
while you Christians go to Jerusalem and argue over the
location of your Prophet. Thus we know our Prophet
lived." The humble missionary replied, "We have no tomb
in our religion, for we have no corpse." The Christian
gospel ends, not in a corpse, but in a Conqueror. It ends
not in a tomb, but in a triumph. "Our gospel is the most
pessimistic of all faiths, in that it dares to look at life
through a cross; but it is the most optimistic of all faiths,
because it looks at life through an Easter morn." And
this is truth.

Immortality is the evergreen of faith. It is incorrupti-
bility; it is exempt from death. Death does not end immortality's day; it only opens it wider. "Death is but a
halting place between two eternities—a gentle wafting to
immortal life." Life began in creation's morning, and
immortality is the completion, the perfection—yea, the
coronation—of God's noble work. The Resurrection is
proof positive of the immortality of the soul. Upon this
faith rests the foundation of the Christian Church. "If
Christ be not risen, then is our preaching vain, and your
faith is also vain." That faith which is "vain" is "empty,"
"futile." But the Church preaches not a "futile" faith.
It preaches a faith which is immortal, which is dynamic,
and the resurrection of Christ—the heart of this faith—
eternalizes the doctrine of the immortality of the soul of
man.

As there were three great mountain-peak experiences in
the life of Moses—namely, Horeb, Sinai, and Nebo, each
dependent upon the other—so the great mountain-peak ex-

periences in the life of our Lord were Transfiguration, Calvary, and Resurrection. Very little is said of the former, but much is said of the last two, especially the last. Peter's faith is couched in these words: "Blessed be the God and Father . . . which according to his abundant mercy hath begotten us again unto a lively hope by the resurrection of Jesus Christ from the dead." When Paul was writing to Timothy, his understudy, he spoke of those things which "are now made manifest by the appearance of our Lord Jesus, . . . who hath abolished death, and hath brought life and immortality to light through the gospel." When the Apostle was writing to the Roman Christians, he urged them "by patient continuance in well doing" to "seek for immortality and eternal life." Jesus announced himself to be "the resurrection and the life" before Resurrection's morning, and encouraged his disciples by assuring them that "he that believeth in me, though he were dead, yet shall he live, and whosoever liveth and believeth in me shall *never die*." This completely eliminates death. Too long has Christendom talked of the "cold, chilly waters," and of a "dark stream," when she might speak of the inviting streams of Life, flowing from the ever-abundant sources of God, upon whose peaceful bosom we shall sail into port at last. There has been too much darkness about our teaching of the future and not enough light; too much sadness and not a sufficient amount of gladness. Recently I stood beside the deathbed of one of God's saints who had lived here, "in service free," for fourscore years and more. That group of devoted loved ones which surrounded the death couch of their beloved were giving her up, *loaning her to God* for his safe-keeping until they met her there. Some one said of the good woman who was fighting her last victorious battle, "When she closes her eyes here, she will open them yonder with God." This dries up the tears of sorrow and mourning and brings the notes of joy and peace. This is the "glass" through which Christians should look.

The hope of immortality is planted deep within the subterranean passages of the mortal breast and is lodged securely within the portals of human experience. Most of the tribes and peoples of the earth have pictured some kind of life after death. This belief in immortality grows as life's development is witnessed and experienced. Many founders of religions have taught the immortality of the soul. Zoroaster, Mahomet, Jesus, and others joined this teaching crusade. Statesmen, such as Cicero, Cromwell, Bismarck, Lincoln, Gladstone, and others, grew eloquent in the expression of their immortal faith. The poets have rejoiced in this field: Homer, Vergil, Dante, Milton, Wordsworth, Tennyson, Browning, and others have made signal contributions in their rippling lines, expressing the soul's faith. The Greeks, in the persons of Plato, Socrates, and Euripides, joined with old Roman Cicero, who spoke his faith in the Senate Chamber, electrifying the atmosphere, as Paul electrified Rome's atmosphere after him. The lines of Shakespeare are filled with immortality's belief, while Victor Hugo, the idol of France, expressed his faith by saying:

> "Winter on my hand,
> Springtime in my heart."

Tennyson took up the harp of life and expressed his grief occasioned by the passing of his friend Hallam, as he looked forward to the immortal realm:

> "Thou wilt not leave us in the dust:
> Thou madest man, he knows not why,
> He thinks he was not made to die;
> And Thou hast made him: Thou art just."

Emerson, standing by his son's grave, gave vent to his emotions and pronouncement of his faith, saying:

> "What is excellent,
> As God lives, is permanent,
> Hearts are dust, hearts' loves remain,
> Hearts' love will meet thee again."

The loves would meet again, and go on forever. The heart of man cries out for something which will not fade, which will not fall. The things of this life of so many ephemeral dreams are falling, fading, disappearing, all around our dwellings, but man cries out, "Give us something which will *endure*." God answered back with "Immortality." It was Whittier who picked up this belief and hope, and expressed it in his "Snow-Bound," saying:

> "Yet Love will dream, and Faith will trust,
> (Since He who knows our need is just),
> That somehow, somewhere, meet we must.
> Alas for him who never sees
> The stars shine through his cypress-trees!
> Who, hopeless, lays his dead away,
> Nor looks to see the breaking day
> Across the mournful marbles play!
> Who hath not learned, in hours of faith,
> 　The truth to flesh and sense unknown,
> That Life is ever lord of Death,
> 　And Love can never lose its own!"

Painters, sculptors, artists, statesmen, poets, musicians, and all who have "walked with unsandaled feet" before this sacred shrine of *faith's immortelle* have endeavored to color, carve, speak, write, and compose as though the productions of the brushes, chisels, tongues, pens, fingers, hearts, and hands were immortal. Hence some productions of art, sculpture, statesmanship, lines of words and strains of music will not cease to live. How impossible to kill Beethoven's Sonatas, or Liszt's Rhapsodies, or Mozart's Symphonies! These creations of the musical heart and the trained mind of man will not perish, if man has his desire. They are composed for the present—and for the future, so far as these artists of the piano are concerned. In such productions we sense a "drive" for immortality. Wilt "Thou leave" these "in the dust"?

If to-day, midst the din and whirl of life, society has come to emphasize the inner manhood and character rather than the outer and bodily conditions, the new estimate of worth is due to the immortal outlook. Since beyond, character is the all-important thing, here also for the sake of manhood men have made great sacrifices. Urged by his friends to polish his writings into perfect form, a great scholar exclaimed, "My books and culture can wait that second life," and so went on serving man. "Ease can wait," said Xavier, toiling for the ignorant. "Pleasure can wait," said Macdonald, toiling in the tenement house district. "Leisure and comfort can wait," said Arnold Toynbee as he served the helpless.

Handel tells us that when he wrote the "Hallelujah Chorus" he saw the heavens opened and all the angels and the great God himself. Because man is to live again, he hath hastened to double his culture and purify it; to double his art and refine it; to ennoble his laws and expel coarseness from his literature and make it divinely beautiful. The immortal outlook has given man all great art, all great work, all great character. For man goes singing, weeping, aspiring, praying through life, journeying not toward a grave in the grass, but toward a statelier Eden. When the little child, the dear mother, the poet, or the statesman falls asleep, could we but look up with Dante, we would see "a divine chariot sweeping through the heavenly confines, its pathway well-nigh choked with flowers."

Beyond the tomb? Yes! More lies beyond the tomb than before the tomb. A cold, crass materialism revolts at such an idea. A seasoned intellect and a Christian heart grasp it. We have endeavored to say that hope and life lie beyond the tomb. I would make a holy trinity by add-

ing to this collection, Victory. These are "beliefs that
matter." The tomb experience was Jesus' greatest victory.
The most signal calamity which could possibly have fallen
to Christianity would have been that of an unresurrected
Lord. Such a Lord would have been a defeated, routed,
beaten Lord. Yea, it would have been more calamitous for
him not to have arisen than for him not to have ever come;
for the resurrection was the test tube, the crucible, of
Christianity's cause. Had he not risen, the Christian
cause would have been a laughingstock. Had he not risen,
man would be still more perfectly wrapped in his selfish
sorrows and keen disappointments; man would yet be
steeped in his unrighteous turmoil and bathed in the hot
tears of false hopes and futile anticipations. Had he not
risen, no faith would beckon us on to greater and more
acceptable accomplishments in life; no noble, high, and
holy ambitions would arise within our once swelling
breasts, or find lodgment within our once expectant
hearts.

The broken, worn, torn, bloody body of the dear Lord
was placed in the tomb with *the hope of victory*. A
wreath of victory was placed on the door of the tomb by
the actions of faithful hands. So much is expressed in
tombstones. A few years ago a group of prominent people
of a Northern city were having dinner together. They
were people of social and financial prominence. Several
of them died tragic deaths within a short time. It was
thought they were poisoned by some of the food which was
eaten. The tomb which rests over the graves of some of
these people is one which speaks of anything else but victory and hope. There is a kneeling woman, prostrate in
her grief, weeping over the graves. Sadness? Surely!
But no hope in that expensive collection of marble. Near
the entrance of another cemetery stands a conspicuous
monument which marks the resting place of somebody's

loved one. Evergreens grow in that cemetery lot. Flowers are there. Hope and victory are expressed in the inscription over the portals of the tomb, "The End of a Perfect Day." The Christian's life is the "end of a perfect day." Jesus' "time" had come. It had come of God. His ending appeared tragic. That was God's way. His rising was triumphant. And that was God's way. Defeat had no part in the occurrences of "the third day." It was routed—routed by Victory's hand.

Dr. S. Parkes Cadman, the "Question Box of the Nation," has on hand, according to a recent announcement, sixty thousand unanswered questions. Sixty-five to seventy per cent of these questions relate to *life beyond the grave.* Man would penetrate the unknown. Some few things of the future are known. Death, which is Life's Window, will open and reveal the rest. Strangely enough, it is death which reënforces our faith in Immortality's victory. Bruce Barton quotes the minister who conducted his mother's funeral as saying: "My whole faith in the integrity and moral reliability of the Universe summons me to a belief that life at its highest, as represented by beautiful and aspiring personalities, was made to go on and not to stop." Maude Royden asserts her faith in this victory in these words: "Nothing that is pure, nothing that is lovely, nothing that is good can die. . . . After life's fitful fever we shall sleep well, and when we wake up after Christ's likeness we shall be satisfied with it." Rabbi Harry Levi quotes John Fiske as saying, "I believe in the immortality of the soul as the supreme act of faith in the reasonableness of God's work." This Rabbi proceeds with his own faith's expression, saying, "I believe in personal immortality, and therefore in personal identity beyond the grave." "For now we see through a glass, darkly; but then face to face; now I know in part; but then shall I know even as also I am known." To-day we see but the baffling reflections.

Then we shall see "face to face." Our loved ones are placed in God's Acre with this hope in our hearts. There is a great comfort to us when we remember that our dear ones are not there in the ground. Our faith has buried them, not in the earth, but in the sky. The grave contains their dust; it cannot house their spirits. They themselves have not tarried here, where dust returns to dust, but have gone on into the Silent Land. They are not dead, but alive —probably far more than we are. This day, called Easter, consecrated to sad memories, is still more *consecrated to immortal hopes*. It points us to the coming time when Memory and Hope and Faith shall strike glad hands with Life's Victory. The uplifted Christ lifts humanity to these summits "where God continually makes 'himself an awful rose of dawn.' "

St. Paul said, "The death that he died, he died unto sin once; but the life that he liveth, he liveth unto God." If we disbelieve these words, human life has no adequate explanation, and admits of none. "Believe them, and you also shall live, in the coherent, meaningful, challenging life of the Spirit, having its dynamic for persistence and the promise of its triumph in the Risen and the Eternal Christ." Cadman says: "If the risen Christ has not satisfied man's quest for life, if all he ever was molders in a Syrian grave, and nothing is left of him but dust and ashes, the darkness that falls on the human race is impenetrable; the riddle of its existence is insoluble; and death, reversing Nature's order here, tyrannizes over life hereafter. Men will not have it so. Deep calls unto deep again in them." "Those who say that the soul at death is blown out like a candle are like the ancient Sadducees," said Dr. Charles E. Jefferson, and proceeds: "They do err, not knowing the Scripture. . . . When we are in fellowship with Him, we walk in the light, and when we are crucified with Him, we have no doubt that we shall rise with Him.

To be sure of immortality *one must live like an immortal.*"
This becomes the privileged experience of that lengthening
stream of Christian devotees who know His Name and
tread on his tracks.

Such privileges, such manifestations, such transactions
are all possible on account of such a Victory. In the gleam
and glow of this Victory we are led into the face, and
through the portals, of the Church's most holy Sacrament.
In the Ritualistic Service the elder prays: "Grant us . . .
so to eat the flesh of thy Son . . . and to drink of his blood
. . . that *we may evermore dwell in him and he in us.*"
The body and blood are presented with the petition that
they may *"preserve thy soul and body unto everlasting
life."* In this hope we are led to believe, with Bishop Edwin D. Mouzon, that "personality in its totality shall be
in true existence as it is here." The general Invitation
and the general Confession speak of a "new life" that is to
result from such a Sacrament. And the elder's petition is
that we might be brought, at last, "unto everlasting life."
The Sacrament teaches us that He still lives, and "we too
shall live." The "emblems" are the outward proof of our
faith that He still lives, and our partaking of them is an
additional assertion of the same faith. Death is struck a
"deathblow" on Easter morning. It is slain in the administration of the Lord's Supper. It is in this faith, and
this faith alone, that we grasp the "torch" which His extended hands have dropped for our acceptance.

XII

IN REMEMBRANCE OF ME

THESE MEDITATIONS were begun purposely with a challenge. They close intentionally with an appeal. A challenge was issued to investigate with renewed interest and interpretation the contents of the Cup. An appeal is made to continue the presentation of these most sacred elements to the parched lips and famished souls of a hungry world. The world is yet hungry for this eternal Food, more so than is sometimes thought. It is more thirsty than is realized. The task of the Church is to study diligently the avenues of approach whereby this Food of immortality and wine of new life may best be presented.

Communion is granting a parting request. Many sorrowful hearts have surrounded the deathbed of a loved one who had only moments to live. The pulse was slow. The eyes were closed in peace. Not a pain passed through the weakened form. The ones who kept the silent vigil had thought that the last words had already been spoken and that unconsciousness had taken hold of the one who was making the last fight; when surely, certainly the lips were seen to move. Those nearest by placed their attentive ears close to the parched, but moving lips, only to hear a parting request: "Don't forget me when I'm gone!" And the soul of the loved one went marching home to its God. But the request? What of it? Did it fall upon listless ears? Did it fail to gain entrance into responsive hearts? No! It was carried out to the letter and with a few sympathetic additions thrown in. The execution of that dying petition, which rang with Christian clarity, was fulfilled to its perfection.

Go once more with me to the Upper Room. Jesus is there, with the hush of his family round him. As the Meal is spread the Master of men makes a parting request. The majority of the group—the large majority—would give it appreciative response. Only one failed to grant it. Here are the words of the Master: "This do in remembrance of me." Here, as much as in any other act of our Lord, we see his humanity, his striking humanity, manifesting itself in the human desire not to be forgotten. On the Cross his humanity flamed with divinity. In the Supper room the humanity of his request takes precedence. Can we blame him for not wanting to be forgotten? Who is there among us who desires to be obliterated from the memories of man? He made a plea for forgetfulness—and it in his own favor. He knew that if it were granted, not only would *he* be remembered, but *we* would be helped. In Paul's letter to the Church members at Corinth he made mention of this parting request of our Saviour, and the marginal reading is: "This do for a remembrance." Many memorials are erected for show. The Memorial of Jesus was erected for service. Many are erected for display. That of Jesus was erected for discipleship.

Yonder upon the lonesome sweeps of old Horeb a man receives his call to service. With the glow of the summons of God in his heart, the Creator assisted in the erection of a tablet there with this inscription upon it: "This is my memorial unto all generations." The memorial explains the deliverance of God's people from the yoke of serfdom round their necks. "On Jordan's stormy banks" twelve men were selected to take twelve stones out of the river. When the following generations, seeing them, would ask, "What mean ye by these stones?" the direct answer could be sent back, "These stones shall be for a memorial unto the children of Israel forever." And they are! Children—and adults—have asked, "What is the meaning of the Communion?"—"What mean ye by *these* stones?" The explanation, which was, and is, in the life of Jesus, rests within the life of the Church. The Psalmist rejoiced that his enemies did not overtake him, and said, in his spiritual glee, "Their memorial is perished with them." The Memorial of Jesus did not "perish" with him. Its eternity reaches its explanation in man's tenacious memory. The Psalmist again gave vent to his emotion, saying, "Thy name, O Lord, endureth forever; and thy memorial . . . throughout all generations." If his memorial endures, the Church will have to be held responsible for its endurance.

Once again the Psalmist exclaimed, "If I forget thee, O Jerusalem, let my right hand forget her cunning." The right hand possessed powers, might, influence; but if one should forget Jerusalem, the choice possession of the right hand must be forgotten. Communion is the "right hand" of the Church. Can it be forgotten? Shall it be forgotten? Isaiah asked, "Can a woman forget her sucking child, that she should not have compassion on the son of her womb?" The prophet here raises the question of the possibility of forgetfulness from the close, intimate maternal standpoint. Could such be a possibility? But he exclaims, "Yea, they may forget, yet will I not forget thee." Here is a portrait of the interest and the tenderness of God. Can such be paralleled in human activity? The Sacrament is the child of the womb of the Church! Can the Church ever forget her fondling, her offspring, the Child of her bosom? My untroubled faith says "No!" The Sacrament will always be preserved, as long as faithful communicants kneel at communion altars. But will it be preserved in its richest contributions and the beauty of its spiritual simplicity? The answer is with the Christian Church.

The little blue flower, called the forget-me-not, is a symbol of constancy. According to an old German tradition, it received its name from the last words of a knight who was drowned in an attempt to procure this little flower for his "lady." The forget-me-not has curled, flowering stems, which unroll as the flowers mature. It has a five-cleft calyx; also its corolla is closed with five scales. This might suggest the five wounds of our Lord, in his hands, in his feet, and in his side. The name of the forget-me-not is the same in all languages of Europe, and it is everywhere the emblem of Friendship. In the language of flowers it stands for Remembrance. This tiny flower has ever been a favorite among poets. So spake Longfellow:

"Silently, one by one, in the infinite meadows of heaven
Blossomed the lovely stars, the forget-me-nots of the angels."

It is possible that "The Little Blue Flower" of Van Dyke was the forget-me-not. In the face of this flower we can see a picture of the Sacrament. For is not the Sacrament an Emblem of Friendship—friendship between God and man? Is it not an emblem of Constancy and an emblem of Remembrance? Yea, it is God's most beautiful Forget-Me-Not in the garden of his flowers of varied hues and aromas.

If the Sacrament was worthy of a genesis, it is infinitely worthy of a perpetuation. That which is perpetual "endures forever." It needs not to be salvaged, for it has not been shipwrecked; but it needs to be continued and kept. Christian devotion is the guarantee of perpetuation. See what went into the Sacrament. Can man ever forget such a life, such a light, such a lift, or such a love? Can we ever forget such a passion, such a Person, such a Power, or such a persuasion? Can such a trial, such Truth, such travail, or such a triumph ever be forgotten? How could such a Sacrifice, such a Sufferer, such a Saviour, or such a Supper ever fail of remembrance? Could ever such a career, such a crusade, such a cross, such a crucifixion, or such a crown as were His be failed to be remembered? His devotion, His denial, His death stand out before the world to-day in bold remembrance. All these experiences of our Master are contained in the Communion. Man's mind, and man's heart, will not let them pass on by with the "wrecks of time." He holds them sacred and secure. He clutches them firmly and fondly unto the bosom of his spiritual possession. In these experiences of Christ lie the only hope of man. The Christian ascends upon their wings of hope, and lives on their daily nourishment. Communion is the Agency of his spiritual crusade. Its perpetuation is not guaranteed in its mere repetition, but in its vital presentation and its inward acceptance. These are its security, and these alone.

> "See, from his head, his hands, his feet,
> Sorrow and love flow mingled down!
> *Did e'er such love and sorrow meet,*
> Or thorns compose so rich a crown?"

"The Forgotten Man" is a term which Methodism uses to describe the retired minister who has been forgotten by the Church. The term is a pathetic, but a truthful one. "The Forgotten Supper" is a sadder term. Its more attractive presentation has been neglected, and man's participation has also been neglected. (See Chapter IV, "The Challenge of the Chalice.") This Service not only looks backward, but its vision is forward—forward toward a new wine of fellowship; forward toward a new kind of Christian kindredship; a relationship which will cause the Christian nations of the world to "beat their swords into plowshares . . . and learn war no more," and live like brothers.

Standing before Saint Peter's, a scholarly professor of an Italian university, in his thrilling lecture on Rome and her past glories, used the words *"we* Christians." But "we Christians" came miserably short of a *Christian* ideal back in that catastrophe which wrecked a world, and from which we have not yet recuperated. There are memorials all over the world to commemorate bloodshed and sacrifice, gore and glory; victories to commemorate battles and bullets, shrapnel and shells. France is dotted with war memorials in the form of national cemeteries, over which the flag of the nation whose dead heroes rest beneath its encircling and protecting folds sways in the hope and heart throb of a warless world. In a hurried moment Mr. Rudyard Kipling wrote his "Recessional," which carries a message for a world which talks much of war, yet continues its manufacture of chemicals that would wipe out an army in a week's time, or less.

> "The tumult and the shouting dies—
>   The captains and the kings depart;
> Still stands *thine ancient sacrifice,*
>   An humble and a contrite heart!
> Lord God of hosts, be with us yet,
> Lest we forget, *lest we forget!*
>
> Far-called our navies melt away,
>   On dune and headland sinks the fire;
> Lo! all our pomp of yesterday
>   Is one with Nineveh and Tyre!
> Judge of the nations, spare us yet,
> Lest we forget, *lest we forget!*"

Possibly the peace workers of the world have not thought of it, and thus have not mentioned it, but the solution of war problems, of peace problems, lies in the inner shrines of the Sacrament. Christendom communes, and then acts like beasts in search of fresh blood. The blood which war-thirsty "Christians" (?) need is that which was spilt on Calvary. Its streams can make a world clean from its hatred, and save it from its jealousies and rivalries, until that dream for which we have long petitioned may come to a fulfillment, "peace shall cover the world as the waters cover the sea." A communing Christian world—one which partakes according to the pattern of the Original—will eventually develop into a warless world.

The Sacrament hovers around a Memorial Table, with Christ as its Centrality. It is the first real Peace Table of the world. He who, pitifully so, caused discord soon vanished from the scene. But the Peace Table remained intact. He did not carry It with him, nor any of Its contents. The story of the signing of the Armistice at the close of the World War is rather familiar to all who kept in touch with the interesting proceedings during those hopeful days. The scene of this epochal occurrence lies in the forest of Compiegne, only a short distance from Paris. Two hastily laid railway tracks were made into the dense mass of that forest: one for the German powers, the other for the Allied powers. The German officials, blindfolded as they were, were led from their own car to the car in which sat the Allied officials. This car in which these representatives met is standing in that forest to-day. The places which were occupied by the various officers which sat around that armistice table are marked. Some wealthy American bought the car and placed is there as a memorial. In the center of the square is a large stone, upon which is carved in deep letters, in the French language, these words:

> "NOVEMBER 11, 1918
> HERE DIED THE CRIMINAL
> PRIDE OF THE
> GERMAN EMPIRE, VANQUISHED
> BY THE FREE PEOPLES
> SHE TRIED TO
> ENSLAVE"

In the Palace of Versailles is the Hall of Mirrors, in which sat the representatives of the nations which had been at war with each other. The purpose of that gathering was the writing of the terms of peace. The ideals of those terms had been conceived within the heart and mind of

America's chief representative, a peace dreamer, a peace devotee, a peace crusader, and, later, a casualty of the World War. Passing through that hall, in vain I looked for the green table which Woodrow Wilson and others had made historic. It was later to be found in a smaller room, removed from the path of tourist traffic. The French lecturer was asked, "Why is the peace table placed behind chains?" Said he, "Sir, you Americans, souvenir hunters as you are, were chipping and cutting it away, and we were forced to place it there for protection and preservation."

There is another Table which rests within the sanctuaries of Christendom. It is not behind chains, neither has it been chipped away by the Christian souvenir hunters of the world. Upon its surface are written these simple words, carved deeply, "In Remembrance of Me." "The criminal pride" of a nation, nor of an individual, lieth not there. Neither was there an endeavor toward *enslavement* in that Memorial which gave us this Table. There was no enmity there. No *proud* victory there. No evil feeling, nor sense of human triumph there. It simply is a peace Table, given to the world for the purpose of *obtaining* personal soul peace and *retaining* world peace. Had there been more of the ideals of the first Table written into the peace terms of the Versailles table, much of the discussion now going on of "the next war" would never have been heard. The "old powers" of the Old World would not listen to Mr. Wilson's dreams. He thought beyond his age; he dreamed beyond his age; he lived beyond his age. In the words which are carved on the monument which marks the resting place of young Quentin Roosevelt, "he outsoared our night." It was thus that America's peace dreamer went to an untimely grave. But he was not the first dreamer of peace who went to a grave before his work was done. The dreams of Jesus were the dreams and ideals of peace— but his work was "finished." We are to "carry on."

It was Stanley Jones—mystic soul that he is, keen mind that he possesses—who called the Communion Table "the most sacred Round Table." And it is! If a modern Church which draws off from hardship and cross-bearing is ever to receive the inner interpretation of this last great Memorial, she must be willing to do some pioneering and some sacrificing. When Canova, the sculptor, was about ready to begin work upon his statue of Napoleon, it is said that his keen eye saw a tiny red line running through the upper part of the block of marble out of which the statue was to be carved. The stone had been brought at great expense from Paris for this express purpose. Common eyes saw no flaw in it, but the sculptor saw it and would not use the marble. If there are flaws in the marble of the life of Christian people to-day—and there are flaws, too many of them—God has a hard time using such material. In "The Challenge of Lent" there is a severe, yet justifiable, arraignment, given by Dr. Joseph Fort Newton: "What fills me with a deep disquiet about Christianity of to-day, both liberal and orthodox, is that it is so harmless. It is so tame, so timid, so tepid; a kind of a glorified lollipop." Too much of the Christianity of to-day is so nonchalant, filled with a spirit of passivity, steeped with an unjustifiable calmness, and immersed beneath an abundance of docility. The sin of indifference rests like a fog over too much of the Church of this day. The call to Communion altars will push back this fog. The rays which come from this Supper room are sufficiently penetrable to clear the path of spiritual progress, for deeper depths, higher heights, and greater victories in the name of Him who said, "Please don't forget me!" Our religion has lost so much of its passion, thus have we lost the passion of Christ, and "if the passion of Christ within us is absent, it is because the preëminence of Christ over us is defective." This "passion" can be found in the rediscovery of Christ. What a hopeful sign it is that this age is rediscovering Jesus; that he is the best Subject for biography and history. Jesus "belongs to the ages," and he cannot be forgotten. This is the hope of the remembrance and obedience of his parting request.

In an obscure church, S. Lorenzo, in Lucina, Italy, is to be found the most wonderful painting of the crucifixion, perhaps, in all the world. It is by Guido Reni. It represents the dying Saviour as a strong young man in the death throes. It is the only portrait that adequately portrays Jesus as a virile man, not effeminate. It is said that the artist stabbed and choked a strong young man and watched him slowly die, in order to get the exact reaction of the facial muscles in the death agony. These he reproduced in this Crucifixion. Guido Reni was sentenced merely to three months' imprisonment for this crime, the judge avowing that his masterpiece of art would atone for the balance. How cheap was life! But what a painting! When the modern Church keeps this picture before the vision of her heart, she will produce virile Christians, who will not remind a man of "glorified lollipops." The death agony which the artist saw can best be visioned in the Sacrament, which has in its background, in its foreground, and in its heart, a cross.

In the Tennessee Conference there used to minister a blind preacher of the glorious gospel. When he was stricken blind, he moped around the house for days and weeks until God got hold of his heartstrings and sent him out to "do the work of an evangelist." He came to my town, and to my church. His face, tender and whitened, possessed a seraphic appearance. He always, so far as I knew, dressed in black. His voice was of unusual kindness. His message was of particular simplicity and carried with it an intensely strong appeal. And when this blind preacher, Brother Joe Ramsey, gave "the call," he would always say, "Let's have our song." That song was, day in and day out, the same song of penetrating, appealing invitation. The hymn was written by Charlotte Elliott, an invalid for fifty lengthy years, one which was written, not for publication, but for the expression of her own spiritual experience—a song which "stole out from her quiet room into the world, where now for sixty years it has been sowing and reaping till a multitude which only God can number have been blessed through its message." The invitation of "Brother Joe" was "Sister Charlotte's" testimony:

> "Just as I am, without one plea,
>   But that thy blood was shed for me,
>   And that thou bidd'st me come to thee,
>   O Lamb of God, I come!
>
> Just as I am, poor, wretched, *blind;*
>   Sight, riches, healing of the mind,
>   Yea, all I need in thee to find,
>   O Lamb of God, I come!"

It was at a children's service one Sunday afternoon when this humble servant of God gave his invitation, and I *accepted it*. That sight flings across the windows of my indelible memory to-day, and the tender entrance of the silent Guest is felt with renewed power and with the richness of a more mature Christian experience, gained down through the years. Forget it? "Can a mother forget her child?" It holds! It keeps! It satisfies! And the revelations of the oncoming years shall tend to better perfect this cherished experience gained in youth's gleaming, beaming childhood. In the remembrance of this experience I am led to better remember Him who said, "Remember me." How can the Church of Christ do any less and profess any degree of loyalty?